**Research Report**

July 2007

CONSORTIUM ON CHICAGO SCHOOL RESEARCH AT THE UNIVERSITY OF CHICAGO

# What Matters for Staying On-Track and Graduating in Chicago Public High Schools

A Close Look at Course Grades, Failures, and Attendance in the Freshman Year

Melissa Roderick, Jenny Nagaoka, Vanessa Coca, Eliza Moeller
*with* Karen Roddie, Jamiliyah Gilliam, and Desmond Patton

## Acknowledgements

The authors gratefully thank their research colleagues at the Consortium on Chicago School Research for advice and helpful suggestions from early to final stages of this work. We would particularly like to thank Steve Ponisciak for his thorough technical reading of the report. Penny Sebring, Melissa Roderick, and Holly Hart reviewed earlier drafts. Staff at the Chicago Public Schools and Consortium Steering Committee members helped develop the major themes in this study. We particularly thank Steering Committee members Arie van der Ploeg and Josie Yanguas for their comments on our work. Two external reviewers, Valerie Lee, University of Michigan, and Tom Hoffer, NORC at the University of Chicago, carefully examined the statistical analyses and provided extensive feedback. Finally, we very gratefully acknowledge the Chicago Public Schools for providing us the data that allowed us to do this work.

This work was supported by grants from the Carnegie Corporation of New York, the John D. and Catherine T. MacArthur Foundation, and the Spencer Foundation.

# Table of Contents

Introduction .................................................................................. 1

Chapter 1: A Close Look at Course Grades, Failures, and Absences
in the Freshman Year ................................................................... 3

Chapter 2: What Matters for Grades and Failure in the Freshman Year:
Student Backgrounds and Behaviors ............................................ 15

Chapter 3: What Matters for Grades, Failure, and Attendance:
School Practices ......................................................................... 25

Chapter 4: Interpretive Summary ................................................ 37

References .................................................................................. 45

Appendix A: *Individual School Data* .......................................... 48

Appendix B: *Description of Survey Measures* ............................. 53

Appendix C: *Correlations Involving Survey Measures* ................ 56

Appendix D: *Summaries of Models* ............................................ 59

# Introduction

Improving graduation rates and reducing dropout rates are high-priority items on the national agenda for high school reform. There is increasing recognition that a high school diploma is a minimum requirement for success in the workplace and that too few students obtain this minimum standard.[1] Yet, it is a problem that can sometimes feel overwhelming to try to manage. In part, this is because of the magnitude of the problem: nationally, nearly one-third of students do not graduate from high school.[2] Almost half the Chicago Public Schools (CPS) students fail to graduate from high school, and in some CPS high schools more students drop out than graduate.[3] These numbers underscore the urgency of addressing this issue immediately.

The dropout problem is also difficult to manage because its causes are many and complex. Research on dropping out has shown that the decision to persist in or leave school is affected by multiple contextual factors—family, school, neighborhood, peers—interacting in a cumulative way over the life course of a student.[4] This suggests a daunting task for dealing with the problem of dropout—if so many factors are involved in the decision to drop out of school, including experiences outside of school and in early grades, how can any high school effort substantially address the problem?

What is often lost in discussions about dropping out is the one factor that is most directly related to graduation—students' performance in their courses. In Chicago, we have shown that inadequate credit accumulation in the freshman year, which usually results from course failures, is highly predictive of failing to graduate four years later. Research in New York City has shown very similar connections between inadequate credit accumulation and eventual dropping out, and national data confirms this; almost all students who drop out leave school far behind in course credits.[5] As we document here in more detail, success in high school coursework is directly tied to eventual graduation. Knowing that graduation is directly tied with course grades suggests two potential strategies for addressing dropout problems. At the very least, we can use freshman course performance to identify students at high risk of dropping out to target with support and intervention. At the most, if schools and teachers can influence the quality of students' performance in their coursework, then they have a direct lever to affect graduation rates—a lever that should simultaneously improve student achievement.

In this report, we look closely at students' performance in their coursework during their freshman year, how it is related to eventual graduation, and how personal and school factors contribute to success or failure in freshman-year courses. We show that data on course performance can be used to identify future dropouts and graduates with precision, and we compare performance indicators to discern how they might be used for nuanced targeting of students at-risk of dropping out. We examine the factors that contribute to course performance in the freshman year, showing that success in coursework is affected more by what students do while they are in high school than by their preparation for high school and backgrounds. Finally, we provide evidence that teachers and schools matter for how students perform in their courses, and that efforts to reduce dropout rates are consistent with initiatives to address low achievement.

We focus on the freshman year because our prior work, and work by others, has shown that course performance in the freshman year sets the stage for eventual graduation. This report builds on a report we released June 2005 that described and defined the "freshman on-track indicator." In that report, we showed the relationship between being on-track at the end of the freshman year and graduating from high school four and five years later. On-track students had at least ten semester credits (five full-year course credits) and no more than one semester F in a core course by the end of their first year in high school. Students who were on-track at the end of their freshman year were nearly four times more likely to graduate from high school than their classmates who were not on-track.[6]

The original on-track report provided initial evidence that we could use freshman-year course performance to precisely identify future dropouts. While it was a key validation of the on-track indicator, it left a number of unanswered questions: Why is the indicator predictive? Why are students off-track? And what might high schools themselves contribute to students' course performance? Furthermore, that report only examined whether students were making minimal progress in their freshman year, which meant whether they were earning sufficient credits to be on-track for promotion to the tenth grade. But we want students to graduate from high school ready for college and work, which means we should aim for students doing A and B quality work.[7] In this report, we pull apart a variety of indicators of freshman course performance—including students' failures, absences, and overall grades—to learn what matters for a successful freshman year.

---

### Introduction Endnotes

1  E.g., Orfield (2004); Barton (2005); National Association of Secondary School Principles (2005).
2  Swanson (2004).
3  Allensworth (2005).
4  Rumberger (2004); Alexander, Entwisle, and Kabbani (2001).
5  Cahill, Hamilton, and Lynch (2006); National Center for Education Statistics (2007).
6  Research in Philadelphia has also shown that course performance in the eighth and ninth grades can be used to identify dropouts years before they leave school (see work by Robert Balfanz, Ruth Curran Neild, and Lisa Herzog). For example, using detailed records on students, Neild and Balfanz (2005) used attendance and failure in the eighth and ninth grades to identify dropouts in Philadelphia. As in Chicago, they found that test scores were not as predictive of graduation as students' performance in their coursework.

7  As documented in the CCSR report, *From high school to the future: A first look at CPS graduates' college enrollment, college preparation, and graduation from four-year colleges*, students with a GPA lower than a 2.0 are unlikely to enroll in college, and those with a GPA lower than 3.0 are unlikely to obtain a four-year degree. Grades are also very predictive of future earnings (Miller, 1998).

# Chapter 1

# A Close Look at Course Grades, Failures, and Absences in the Freshman Year

As a measure of minimally adequate performance, the on-track indicator groups together marginally successful students and very successful ones. Knowing that the on- and off-track groups both contain students with widely differing course performances, we decided to explore what aspects of being off-track made students less likely to graduate, and if more nuanced indicators of course performance—such as number of course failures, GPA, or absences—might be better predictors of eventual graduation. We begin this chapter by examining these other indicators of course performance as predictors of graduation. We then use the other indicators to look more closely at what it means to be off-track.

## A Number of Freshman-Year Indicators Can Be Used to Predict High School Graduation

The on-track indicator is highly predictive of graduation, but it is a blunt indicator; and the requisite data to construct the indicator are not available until the end of a student's first year in high school. Schools and districts often ask if there are other indicators that could be used to forecast graduation. In fact, there are several related measures of how well students do during their freshman year that are equally predictive and more readily available, including freshman-year GPA, the number of semester course failures, and freshman-year absences.

## Freshman Course Performance Among CPS Students

This report analyzes several different, but related, indicators of freshman-year performance. Each is defined below, along with summary figures that show the performance of first-time ninth-graders in the 2004–05 school year (24,894 students). We include only students who remained in school through spring of their freshman year.

The 2005 report on the on-track indicator showed that freshman-year course performance has improved over the last decade in CPS; on-track rates improved from 50 percent with the 1994–95 freshman class to 60 percent with the 2003–04 class (excluding first-year dropouts), while freshman-course pass rates improved from 76 to 81 percent over the same period.[A] However, as detailed below, one cannot escape the conclusion that, in general, freshmen in CPS still do very poorly; more than half of freshmen fail a course, the average GPA is below a C, and absence rates are very high—40 percent of freshmen miss more than four weeks of school (including class cutting). The statistics would sound even worse if we included freshmen dropouts in the calculations. For many students, freshman year is like a bottleneck—their performance is so poor that they are unable to recover. These negative experiences in freshman year put students at high risk of not graduating, which later prevents them from participating in the mainstream economy and larger society. We cannot hope to substantially improve graduation rates unless we substantially improve students' course performance in their freshman year.

**On-Track:** A student is considered on-track if he or she has accumulated five full credits (ten semester credits) and has no more than one semester F in a core subject (English, math, science, or social science) by the end of the first year in high school. This is an indicator of the minimal expected level of performance. Students in CPS need 24 credits to graduate from high school, so a student with only 5 credits at the end of freshman year will need to pass courses at a faster rate in later years. The definition is aligned with the CPS promotion policy for moving from freshman to sophomore year, which only requires five full credits. In the 2004–05 freshman class, 59 percent of first-time high school students were on-track while 41 percent were off-track (excluding students who dropped out before the end of their first year in high school).

**Number of Semester Course Failures:** In this report, we measure failures across all courses by semester. This differs from the on-track indicator, which only incorporates failures in core subjects (reading, math, science, and social science); this report examines overall course performance, not just performance in core courses. A typical student takes 7 courses each semester; thus, a typical student could fail as many as 14 courses in a year. Figure 1 graphs the number of semester courses failed by first-time freshmen in the 2004–05 school year, excluding students who dropped out before the end of their first year in high school. The modal category of failures is 0; however, more than half the CPS freshmen (53 percent) fail at least one course.

### FIGURE 1
**Number of Course Failures Among Freshmen in 2004-05**

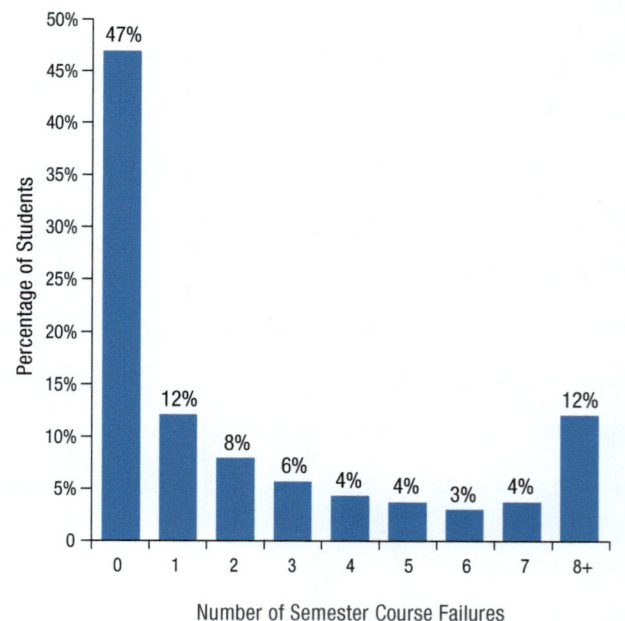

**Grade Point Average (GPA):** CPS students receive a weighted GPA on their report card, which gives extra points for grades in honors and Advanced Placement (AP) courses. In this report, we analyze unweighted GPAs (which use values of 4 points for an A, 3 for a B, 2 for a C, 1 for a D, and 0 for an F) for all credit-bearing classes. We analyze unweighted GPAs rather than weighted GPAs because all students do not have equal access to honors, International Baccalaureate (IB), and AP courses. Figure 2 shows the distribution of GPAs among first-time freshmen in 2004–05, for students who remained in school through spring term. A 2.0 GPA (C average) is typical for CPS freshmen. Very few students—only 3 percent—have A averages their freshman year, while more than 40 percent of freshmen finish the year with a GPA lower than 2.0 (a D+ average or lower). About a quarter of students have a B or higher average at the end of their freshman year.

**Course Absences:** Absences are counted on a course-by-course basis and then aggregated into total number of days absent. If a student misses one out of seven courses in a day, it counts as one-seventh of a day of absence for that student. Figure 3 shows absence rates for students entering CPS high schools in the 2004–05 school year, excluding students who dropped out before the end of their first year in high school. One-quarter of students missed less than one week of school per semester. Forty percent of students missed more than two weeks of school per semester, which is a month or more of class time per year. There are 90 days in each semester, so these students missed more than 10 percent of the annual instructional time. Students can be counted as truant with 20 unexcused full-day absences.

**FIGURE 2**
**Distribution of Freshmen GPAs in 2004-05**

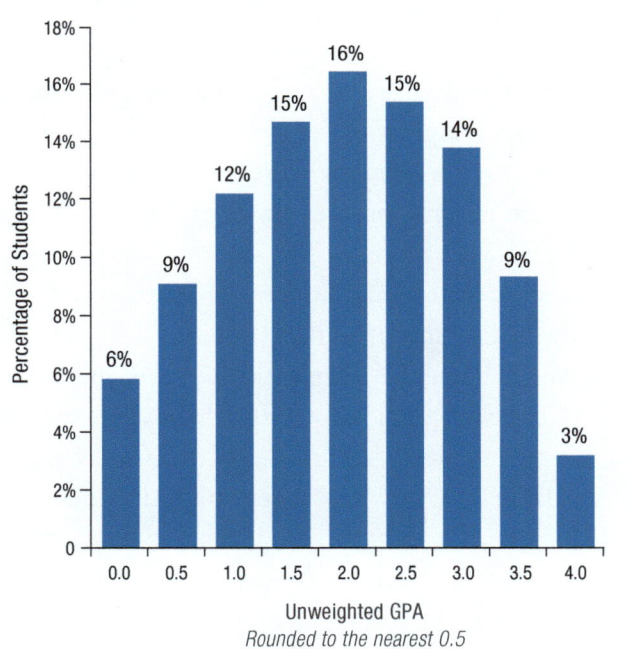

**FIGURE 3**
**Absences Among Freshmen in 2004-05**

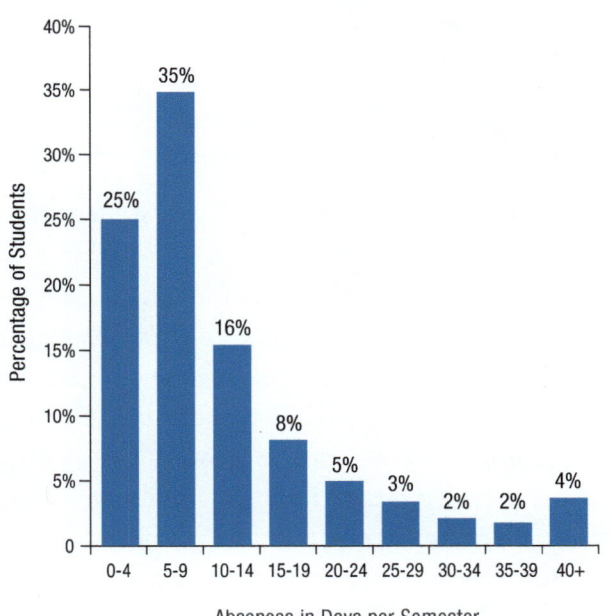

## Sidebar Endnotes
A Allensworth and Easton (2005).

Table 1 shows how well each of the four indicators of freshman-year course performance predicts whether students will graduate from high school within four years. Whether a student is on-track, GPA, and the number of semester course failures all correctly identify graduates and nongraduates 80 percent of the time. GPA is the most accurate for identifying nongraduates. Freshman-year absences are slightly less predictive than the other three indicators because they do not distinguish students who are attending school but performing poorly in their classes from those who are attending and performing well. Although the four indicators of course performance may seem somewhat interchangeable, they each provide somewhat different information, as described below.

**TABLE 1**
**Predictive Ability of Indicators of Freshman-Year Performance**

| Freshman Performance Indicator | Overall Correct Prediction | Specificity *Predicting Nongraduates* | Sensitivity *Predicting Graduates* |
|---|---|---|---|
| GPA | 80% | 73% | 85% |
| On-Track vs. Off-Track | 80% | 72% | 85% |
| Semester Course Failures | 80% | 66% | 89% |
| *Fall-semester failures* | *76%* | *55%* | *91%* |
| Absences | 77% | 59% | 90% |
| *Fall-semester absences* | *74%* | *53%* | *89%* |

In the earlier report, we showed that students on-track at the end of their freshman year are about four times more likely to graduate than off-track students (see Figure 4). The on-track indicator has advantages over the other indicators in terms of ease of reporting and being easily understood by a broad public. Because it is a categorical variable with only two values—either on- or off-track—it is easy to report trends over time. However, the on-track indicator does not provide information that is precise enough to allow specific students to be targeted for specific interventions. In addition, the indicator does not provide timely information to schools: it cannot be calculated until the summer after students' first year of high school.

Several researchers have found that high absence rates are strong predictors of dropping out.[1] In CPS, about 15 percent of first-time freshmen have extremely high absence rates, missing one month or more of classes each semester (see Figure 3). These students have largely disengaged from school—they remain enrolled, but have marginal attendance—and they have less than a 10 percent chance of graduating (see Figure 5). However, it is not just extremely low attendance that is problematic. *Even moderate levels of absences are a cause for concern.* Just one to two weeks of absence per semester, which are typical for CPS freshmen, are associated with a substantially reduced probability of graduating. In the 2000–01 cohort, only 63 percent of students who missed about one week (five to nine days) graduated in four years, compared to 87 percent of those who missed less than one week. This is of great concern, considering that only one-quarter of CPS freshmen miss less than one week of school per semester. Attendance is clearly a vital part of graduating from high school, but beyond this we show evidence later in this report that attendance is the most essential requirement for avoiding course failure.

Information on absences is available early in the school year and might be the most practical indicator for identifying students for early interventions. More than half the nongraduates can be identified by the end of the first semester using either absence or failure rates. By the end of the first term, course grades and failure rates are slightly better predictors of graduation than attendance because they directly indicate whether students are making progress in their courses. These rates also provide more specific information to target programs for struggling students than the on-track indicator. GPA, in particular, provides information about who is likely to struggle in later years and is the best indicator for predicting nongraduates.[2] As shown in Figure 6, students with a 2.5 GPA (C+ average) in their freshman year have a very high likelihood of graduating within four years—86 percent did so in the 2000–01 freshman cohort. As grades fall between 2.0 (C average) and 0.5 (D- average), graduation rates fall dramatically. Just under three-fourths of students with a 2.0 (C average) graduated by 2004 in the 2000–01 cohort, compared to about one-quarter of students with a 1.0 (D average). Virtually no student with an average lower than a D in the freshman year earned a CPS diploma; this is a cause for concern, given that 15

**FIGURE 4**
**Four-Year Graduation Rates by Freshman On-Track Status**

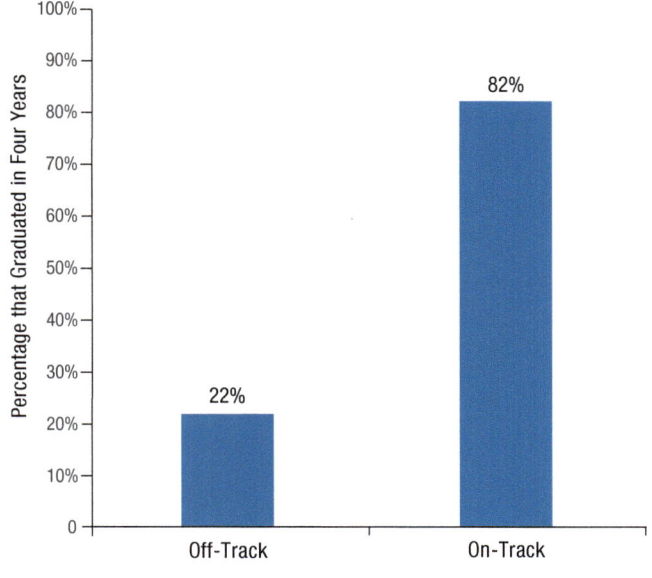

**FIGURE 5**
**Four-Year Graduation Rates by Freshman Absence Rates**

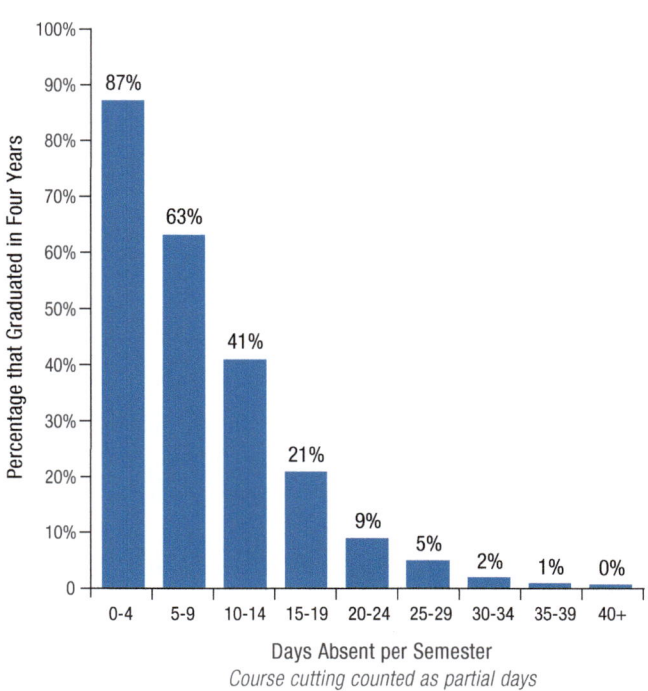

**FIGURE 6**
**Four-Year Graduation Rates by Freshman GPA**

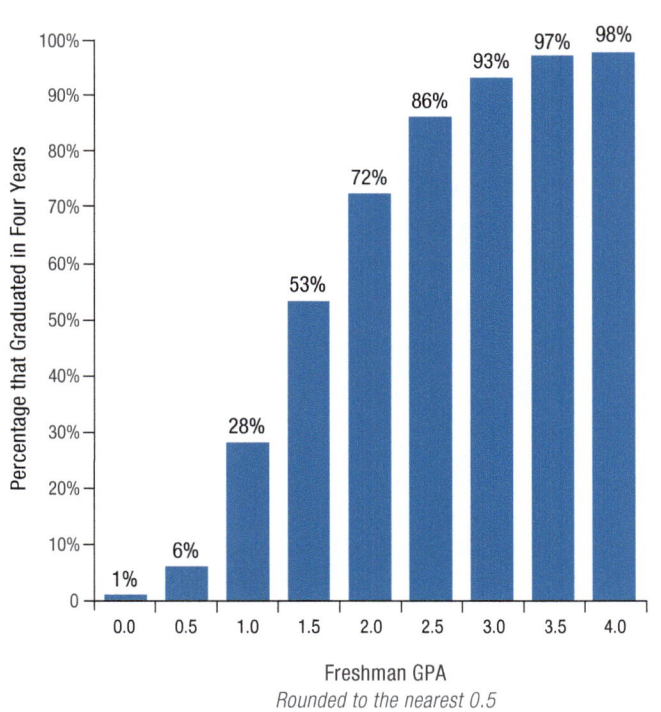

**FIGURE 7**
**Four-Year Graduation Rates by Freshman Course Failures**

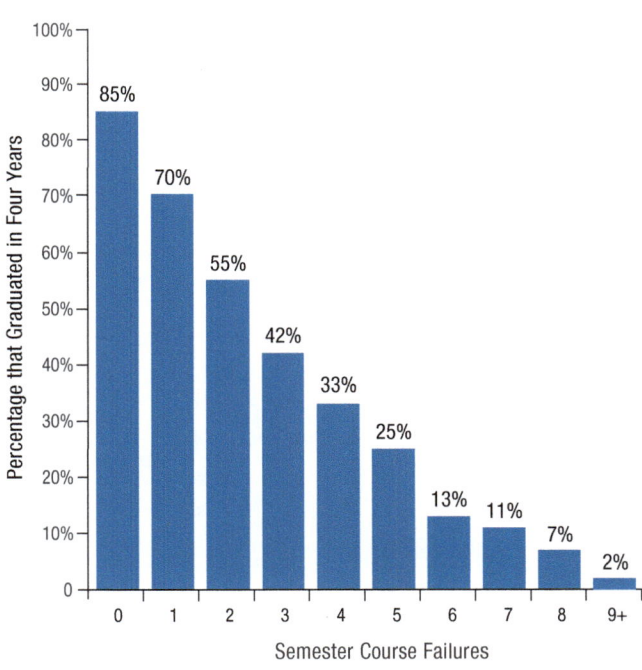

*Graduation rates are based on students entering high school in September 2001, followed until September 2005 for Figures 4-7.*

percent of CPS students finished their freshman year with lower than a D average (see Figure 2).

On the other hand, students with good grades in their first year are very likely to be successful in their remaining years of high school. In the 2000–01 entering class, *almost all students with a B average or higher at the end of their freshman year graduated within four years.* Furthermore, almost 80 percent of these students graduated with a final GPA of 3.0 or higher. We know from research that the decision to drop out is affected by myriad factors in students' lives, many of which exist outside of the school.[3] It is probable that first-year students who earned high grades experienced fewer outside stressors than other students, and fewer personal and home problems undoubtedly made graduating from high school easier for them. However, it is also likely that many of the students who received good grades their freshman year also struggled with problems outside of school sometime during their four years of high school. Remember from Figure 2 that almost a quarter of CPS freshmen have B or higher averages in a district that is about 90 percent low income—thus, most students with B or higher averages are low-income students. Still, 95 percent of the students with B or higher averages graduated within four years.[4] Success in the freshman year may make it easier for students to continue, despite personal and family problems that might develop during the course of high school.

Clearly, GPAs are related to course failures because failures are part of the calculation of students' GPAs. Course failures are more directly tied to graduation, however, because students need to accumulate a specific number of course credits to receive a diploma, and they must pass their classes to obtain credits. This is

## Students' Freshman-Year Course Performance Is Much More Important for Graduation Than Their Background Characteristics and Prior Achievement

Students' likelihood of graduation is affected by their educational experiences prior to high school, and is related to their economic and demographic backgrounds.[A] Research on graduation has shown particularly strong relationships of graduation with students' test scores and age on entry into high school—which is a proxy for grade retention. Graduation is also related to students' gender, race, and economic status. However, all of these factors together explain only about 12 percent of the variation in graduation rates in the cohort of students entering CPS high schools in the 2000–01 school year.[B] In contrast, students' freshman-year GPA and number of Fs explain 39 percent of the variation in graduation rates.[C] Once we know how students performed in their classes in their freshman year, additional information about their backgrounds does little to improve our prediction of whether they will graduate. [D] As we showed in Table 1, ninth-grade Fs or GPA each can be used to predict about 80 percent of graduates; if we include information about students' background characteristics and prior achievement, we only improve the prediction by about half a percentage point.[E]

### Sidebar Endnotes

A  E.g., Rumberger (2004); and Alexander, Entwisle, and Kabbani (2001).

B  This is the reduction in log-likelihood (pseudo-$R^2$) that is achieved by predicting graduation with students' eighth-grade test scores, age, race, gender, poverty, and economic status with a logistic regression model.

C  The variance explained increases from 12 to 40 percent if indicators of freshman course performance are included in the models described in the previous footnote.

D  Background characteristics explain only an additional 1 percent more variation in graduation rates than do freshmen Fs and GPA alone.

E  These statistics on variance explained in dropout are similar, albeit slightly smaller, to those reported by Alexander, Entwisle, and Kabbani (2001) in their comprehensive study of factors across the life-course that contribute to graduation/dropout. They reported that ninth-grade performance, behaviors, and attitudes (GPA, grade retention, parent attitudes, pupil behaviors, and pupil attitudes) together explained 44.1 percent of the variation in dropout rates; when they added in background factors, the variation explained increased by just under 6 percent (to 49.8 percent).

reflected in the consistent relationship between the number of courses a student fails and whether that student eventually graduates, as shown in Figure 7. Each additional course failure makes it more difficult to graduate.[5] Once students have failed six semester courses (i.e., three full-year courses), they are so unlikely to graduate that additional failures only modestly decrease the probability of graduating; these students have failed half their courses or more.[6]

Because each indicator has different advantages, an effective monitoring system could be created to take advantage of each indicator at different points in the school year. For example, because absence rates are known early in the school year, schools could address poor course attendance within the first quarter. After students' first-quarter grades are known, students with failure warnings should receive immediate supports. When semester grades are posted, those students with failures will need a strategy for making up missing credits. At the end of the school year, students' grades could be used to identify students at high risk of future failure and to identify students performing below their potential (e.g., students with high test scores but low grades). On-track rates for the cohort could be determined in the summer after the school year as a simple indicator to evaluate school programs and policies, and to identify particular groups of students with nonpromotion rates that are especially high.

## Course Failure Is a Sign that Students Are Generally Struggling in School

Students can be off-track just by failing one yearlong course (two semester courses). After writing the last report, we wondered about the extent to which students were thrown off-track by an aberrant course failure. We also wondered if course failure was as detrimental to graduation among students who were generally doing well in their other courses as it was for students who were struggling across all of their courses. To gain a better understanding of the variability in the course performance of on- and off-track students, and what that variability means for graduation, we examine on- and off-track performance by students' failures and their grades in the courses they passed.

In general, off-track students are struggling in all of their courses. Figure 8 shows the distribution of GPAs in passed courses by the number of semester course failures. Even on-track students have relatively low GPAs. Among students with no failures, the typical GPA is about 2.5 (C+). Only half (48 percent) has a GPA of a B or higher; 23 percent are C or D+. Among students with only one semester F, who are also on-track by our definition, over 90 percent have a GPA lower than 3.0 (B average) in the courses that they pass. More than three-fourths of students who fail just one full-year course have grades averaging 2.0 or lower (C or lower) in the classes they pass. Almost all off-track students who fail two or more semester courses have GPAs of 2.0 or lower in the classes they pass. It is most typical for off-track students to have a GPA of 1.5 (D+ average) in the courses they pass.

Few students experience isolated problems and perform well in other coursework. Failure in even one semester course is generally a sign of trouble in other courses. This suggests that problems or successes in one class may generalize to other classes. For example, a student who skips one class may fail to show up to subsequent classes that day. Likewise, success in one class may lead a student to put forth more effort in other classes. Of course, performance in all courses will be affected by factors such as students' background and preparation, and by the overall instructional climate of the school.

The strong connection between grades overall and failures in a few classes has implications for how we think about high school reform strategies. *Instead of being isolated, problems with course failure tend to indicate broader problems of academic performance.* This suggests that strategies that address particular courses (e.g., math remediation or tutoring) might be limited in their ability to affect broader outcomes, compared to more comprehensive strategies (e.g., instructional coordination across classes or schoolwide attendance initiatives). This also suggests problems of course failures, dropping out, and low achievement should be addressed by coordinated strategies. These issues are discussed further as we explore the school factors associated with freshman-year course performance.

## FIGURE 8
**Grades in Passed Courses by Number of Course Failures**

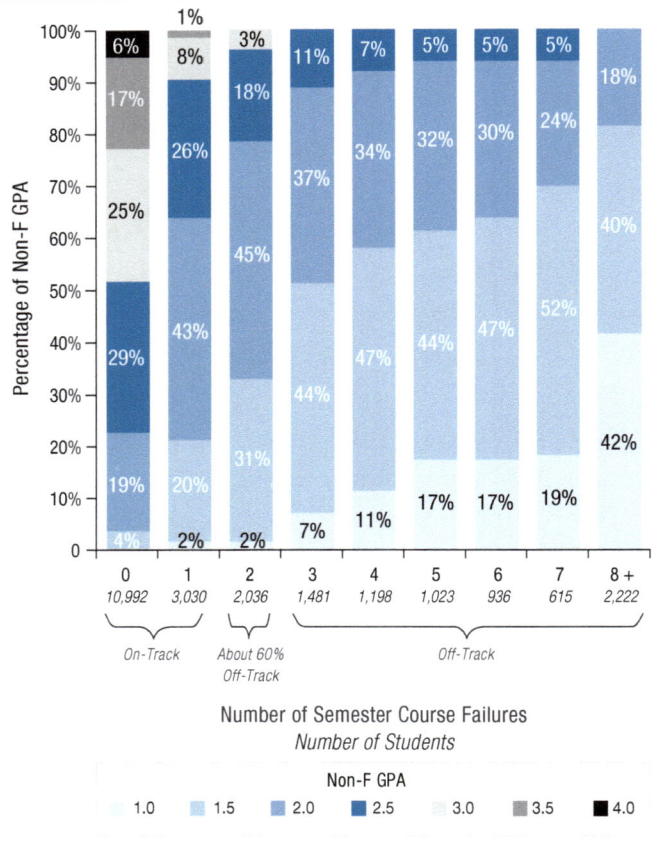

## Overall Grades, as Well as Failures, Matter for Graduation

Course failures and overall GPA are strongly related. However, among students with the same number of Fs, higher grades in other courses increase the likelihood of graduation. Figure 9 shows graduation rates classified by the number of Fs and GPA in the courses that students passed. Each column represents students with the same number of freshman-year failures. Among students with the same number of failures, those who had higher grades in the courses they passed were much more likely to graduate. Even students with no failures in their first year of high school were at some risk of not graduating if they had a C average or lower. It is likely that poor grades in the freshman year foreshadow problems with course failure in later years. Students who just barely pass their freshman classes are likely to struggle as they move into their sophomore year.

Course grades predict the likelihood of graduating, but course failures have a direct effect on graduation beyond their relationship with students' overall grades. Ultimately, students need course credits to

## FIGURE 9
**Graduation Rates by number of Fs and GPA in Passed Courses**

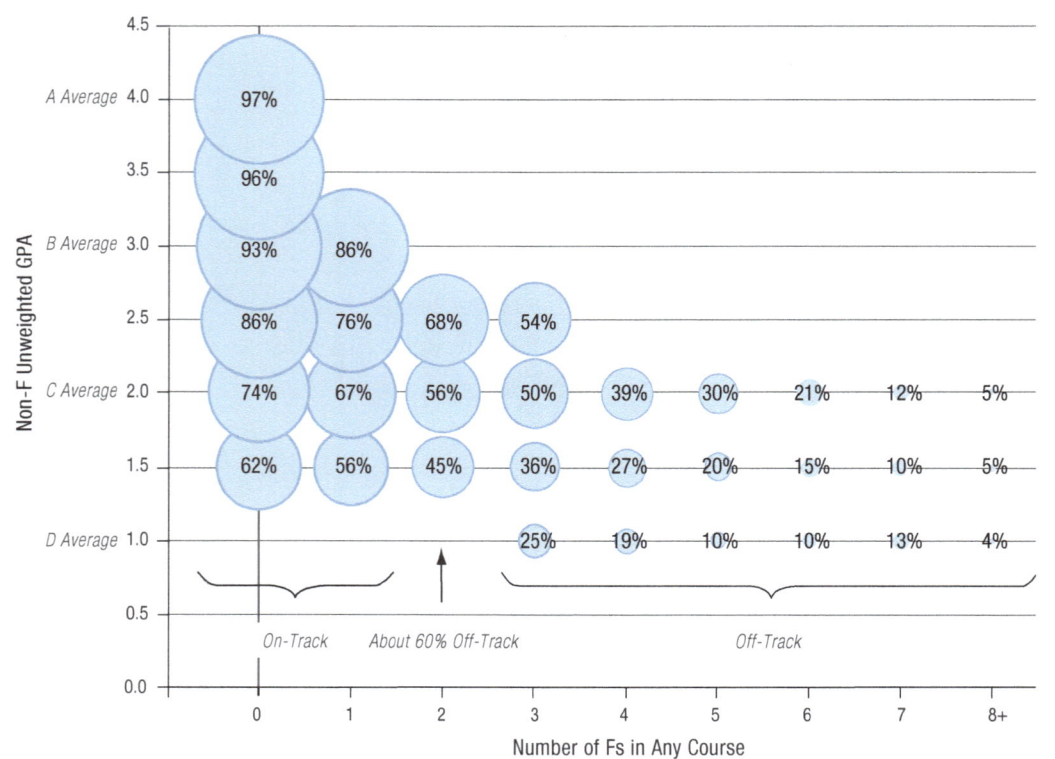

**How to Read this Chart:**
*The size of the bubbles indicates the four-year graduation rate of students entering high school in the 2000-01 school year by their freshman year course failures and grades in the classes they passed. Students who passed all of their courses in their first year of high school are in the first column. Their graduation rates ranged from 62 percent among students with a 1.5 GPA to 97 percent for students with a 4.0. Among students who failed two semester classes their freshman year, graduation rates ranged from 45 percent among students who received a mix of Cs and Ds in the classes they passed (averaging 1.5 points) to 56 percent for students with all Cs in the classes they passed (2.0 average), up to 68 percent for students with a mix of Cs and Bs (2.5 average) in the courses they passed.*

graduate; and failures have a direct effect on the probability of graduating. As shown in Figure 9, the probability of graduating declines quickly with each additional course failure.[7] This can be seen more clearly in Figure 10, which shows graduation rates by freshman GPA for both on- and off-track students. All students with very low freshman GPAs are off-track (see far left of graph), and nearly all students with high GPAs are on-track (see far right of graph). But in the middle range, GPAs from 1.0 to 2.5 (D to C+), students can be either on- or off-track depending on how many Fs they have. For students in this middle range, about 60 percent of students, having failed more than one semester course has a strong impact on the likelihood of graduating. Among students with the same overall GPA, on-track students are about 9 percentage points more likely to graduate than off-track students with the same GPA. This occurs even though off-track students must have had higher grades in their passed courses than students with the same overall GPA who are on-track.

## Intervention Efforts Are Needed for More Than Just the Lowest-Performing Students

Students with high rates of course failure are extremely unlikely to graduate. Those who fail four or more semester courses (i.e., two courses in each semester), or who hold lower than a D average, probably need very intensive assistance in order to graduate; and schools may be disappointed with the effects of programs that are not sufficiently comprehensive. On the other hand, students with GPAs in the D+ or C- range, or just one failure in the first semester (two semester failures for the year), are about as likely to graduate as not to graduate. Because students in this GPA range constitute a large percentage of students and they have a reasonable chance of graduating, efforts to support these students could have a substantial payoff for school graduation rates. However, because such students are not the lowest performers, these students may not be seen as in great need of support.

To gauge the degree to which graduation rates might be affected by a targeted effort to increase passing

**FIGURE 10**

**Percentage of Students Who Graduated in Four Years by Freshman GPA and On-Track Status**

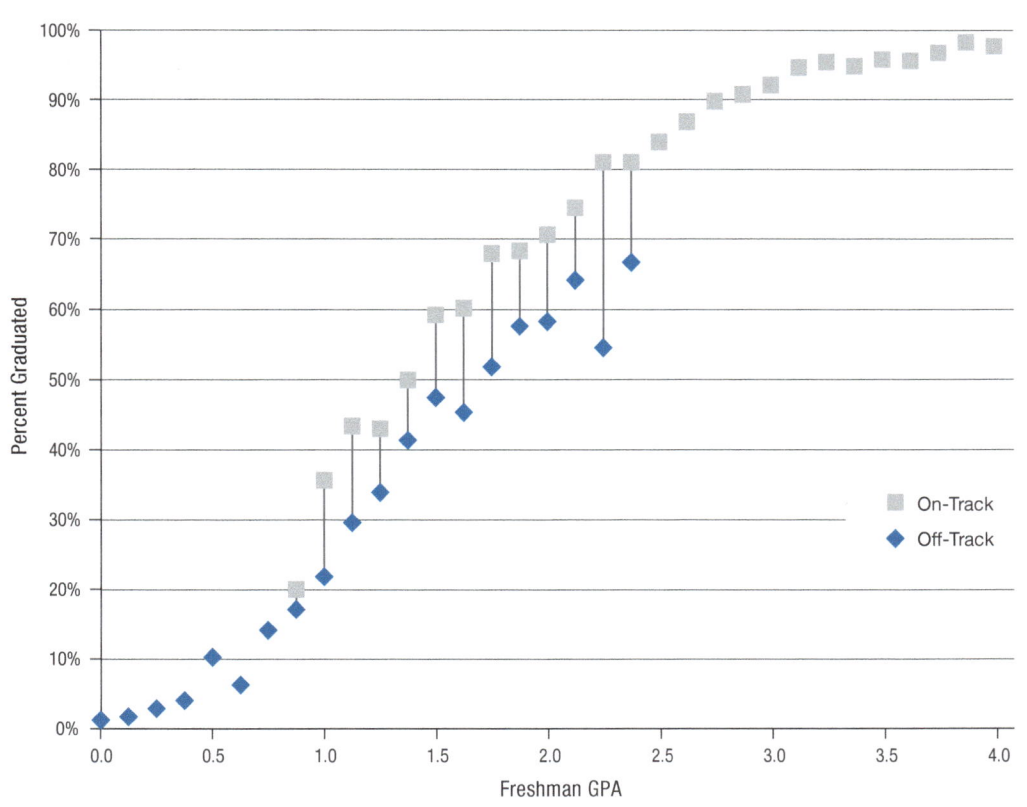

*Almost all students with GPAs below 1.0 are off-track, while almost all students with GPAs above 2.5 are on-track. Students with GPAs of 1.0 to 2.5 may be either on- or off-track. The gray lines show the difference in graduation rates for students with the same GPAs by on-track status. Students who are off-track must have had higher grades in the courses they passed than on-track students with the same GPA, yet they are about 9 percentage points less likely to graduate.*

rates, Figure 11 simulates the maximum improvements in graduation rates that could be expected if schools could find a way to get each student to pass two additional semester courses (one full-year course) in their freshman year. This could be considered a summer school recovery effect, since students can take a full-year course over the summer, or a potential effect of increasing academic supports in the school year. To estimate the effect, we simply assign each student the graduation rate observed among students who had two fewer failures than that student. This is an overestimation of potential graduation rates, because we do not consider other factors that are associated with failure that influence graduation. However, it allows us to gauge the relative effects of improvements in pass rates on different groups of students.

The bottom of Figure 11 shows that about half the students who entered CPS high schools in 2000–01 and failed to graduate four years later received multiple Fs in their freshman year: 2,679 students who failed to graduate had seven or more semester Fs in their freshman year, and an additional 1,347 students who failed to graduate had five or six semester Fs. Thus, this may seem like a reasonable group to target for recovery efforts or tutoring. However, improving pass rates among these students by two semester courses would do little to affect overall graduation rates—their probability of graduating is so small that they would still be unlikely to graduate with an additional two course credits. We might expect as many as 170 additional graduates among students with seven or more semester failures (a 1 percentage point increase in the total graduation rate), and as many as 308 more graduates among students with five or six semester course failures (a 2 percentage point increase in the total graduation rate). Students with many course failures will need more support than tutoring or summer school to have a reasonable chance of graduating—all of these students

**FIGURE 11**

**Estimated Improvements in Systemwide Graduation Rates if Each Student Passed Two Additional Semester Courses***

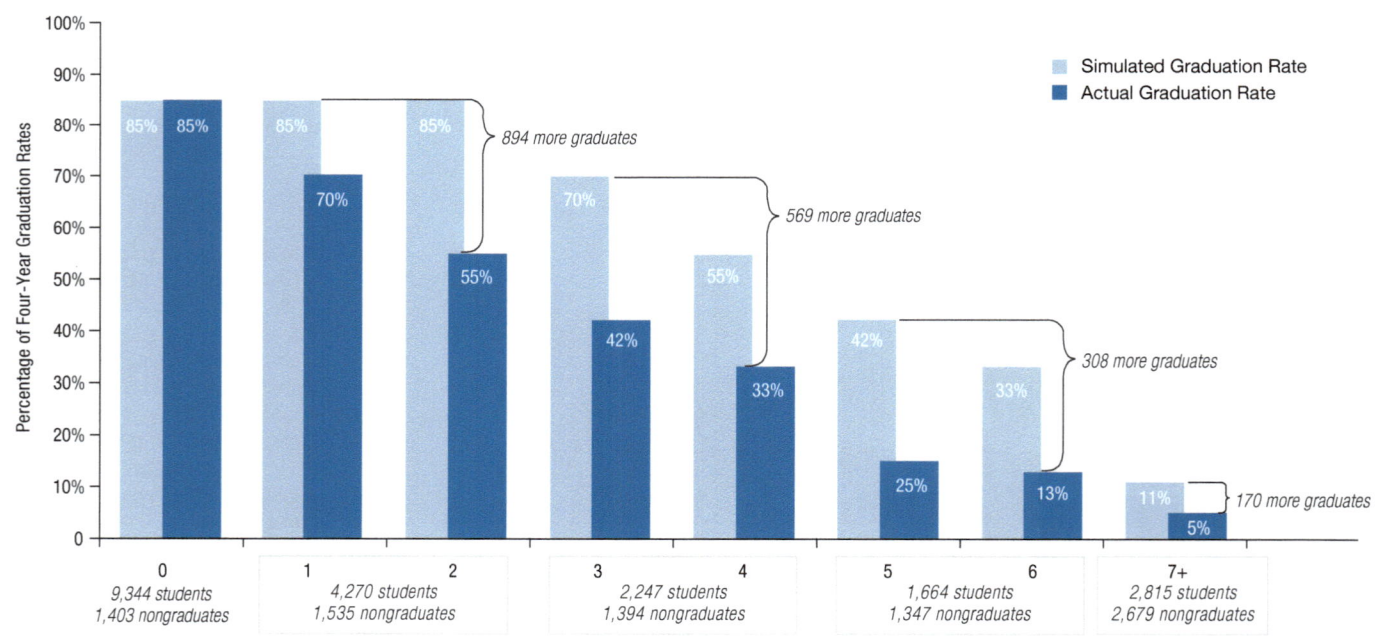

*Graduation rates for students failing fewer than two courses are estimated as if they failed no courses. This simulation suggests the maximum degree to which graduation rates could be expected to improve if each student failed two fewer courses or recovered two courses immediately after failure. It is an overestimation because it does not take into account factors other than Fs that affect graduation (e.g., grades in passed courses tend to be lower among students with more Fs). However, it can be used to gauge the relative effects of recovery or improvements in pass rates for students with different rates of failure. While students with multiple Fs comprise the majority of nongraduates, small improvements in pass rates or recovery among these students would have a much smaller effect on graduation rates than similar efforts among students who have failed only one or two courses. These figures are based on students in the 2000-01 freshman cohort.

## How We Obtained Information on Students and Schools

The analyses in this report are based on two cohorts of students. The statistics that show freshman course performance without any reference to graduation rates or survey data are based on all freshmen who entered CPS high schools in fall 2004 who did not attend charter schools (24,894 students). Statistics that tie freshman course performance to graduation rates are based on all students who entered CPS high schools in fall 2000 who did not transfer out of CPS before September 2004 and who did not attend a charter school (20,803 students).[A] Statistics that use survey data only include those students from the 2004–05 cohort who participated in the spring 2005 surveys (14,045 students) described below.

Data on students' course absences and grades come from semester-by-semester grade files provided by the Chicago Public Schools (CPS). Data on grades and absences are provided separately for each course taken by each student each semester. All CPS schools, except charter schools, provide this information. For this reason, charter school students cannot be included in any of the analyses in this report.

Data on students' background characteristics and school demographics come from student administrative records and test score files provided by CPS. Gender, race, and age are part of the administrative record files. Mobility, which is calculated from longitudinal administrative records on individual students, is measured as the number of times a student changed schools in the three years prior to high school. Eighth-grade achievement is measured with students' scores in the reading and math sections of the Iowa Tests of Basic Skills (ITBS).

Students' socioeconomic status is measured through two variables, which were constructed from the 2000 U.S. census data, regarding the economic conditions in students' residential block groups. The first, concentration of poverty, is constructed from information on the male unemployment rate and the percentage of families living below the poverty line. The second, social status, is constructed from information about average income and education levels. These indicators allow for much more discrimination in socioeconomic background than the simple indicator of free/reduced lunch, for which about 90 percent of CPS students are eligible.

Measures of school climate come from surveys conducted by the Consortium on Chicago School Research (CCSR) in spring 2005. Nearly 130,000 students, teachers, and principals across the system participated. Our surveys ask about learning climate, teacher-student relationships, leadership, and quality of the school's instructional program. They also ask about the school's professional environment, and the nature of the school's relationships with parents and the community. From these surveys we create measures about features of each school.[B] Students' perceptions of climate are constructed from responses of ninth- and tenth-grade students. Teachers' perceptions are constructed from responses of teachers at all grade levels.

Unfortunately, the data do not allow us to discern individual students' specific experiences on a class-by-class basis. For each measure, students either reported on just one of their courses (English or math) or on the school as a whole. We can aggregate the data from all students to create measures of climate across the school, and classroom climate across English and math classes in the school, but we cannot distinguish different patterns of experience within the school among different students. Still, these measures of the average climate in schools provide some evidence about what matters for course performance, although we would expect to find stronger relationships if we could map out different experiences within schools.

### Sidebar Endnotes

A  Students who left for involuntary reasons (incarceration, institutionalization, death) are excluded from analyses, along with those who transferred out of CPS.

B  For more information on our surveys and on the psychometric properties of our measures, visit the CCSR Web site at ccsr.uchicago.edu.

need to pass *at least* four additional semester courses to be on-track, and many need much more. Modest efforts to support these students will not be sufficient to have a sizable impact on graduation rates.

On the other hand, summer school and tutoring that is targeted at students with small numbers of course failures could potentially have a sizable effect on graduation rates. If students who failed just one or two semester classes were to pass those classes instead of failing them, we might expect as many as 894 additional graduates. If students who failed just three to four semester classes (up to two full-year classes) were to pass an additional two semester classes (one full-year class), we might expect an additional 569 more graduates. Together, this is a 7 percentage point increase in the overall graduation rate. It is also likely easier to improve pass rates among students with few Fs than among students with multiple failures.

### Chapter 1 Endnotes

1  E.g., Balfanz and Neild (2006); Alexander, Entwisle, and Horsey (1997).
2  In fact, 86 percent of nongraduates can be identified with freshman GPA by sacrificing specificity to 68 percent.
3  Rumberger (2004a); and Alexander, Entwisle, and Kabbani (2001).
4  Ninety-five percent of these students graduated within four years, and only 3 percent dropped out. The remaining 2 percent remained for a fifth year of high school.
5  Besides preventing credit accumulation, failure may also impede graduation through indirect mechanisms. For example, failure may demoralize students and lower their expectations. Failure may also disrupt students' schedules when they need to repeat a failed class. Often students progress to classes that build on knowledge that should have been learned previously, thus a failure can indicate that a student is unlikely to succeed in a future class. For example, most CPS students who fail algebra in their freshman year take geometry in their sophomore year before passing algebra.
6  Most students take seven courses in their first year of high school.
7  Each additional course failure decreases the probability of graduating by about the same amount as a decrease of half of a grade point across all classes.

# Chapter 2

# What Matters for Grades and Failure in the Freshman Year: Student Backgrounds and Behaviors

Why do some students make a successful transition to high school while others fail? Is freshman course performance mostly a result of students' backgrounds and preparation in elementary school? Is performance influenced by where students go to school or by factors that are in the control of teachers and school professionals? In this chapter, we begin to address these questions by examining the student factors associated with course absences, failures, and grades. In a subsequent chapter, we bring in the characteristics of schools.

## Attendance Is Crucial for Passing Classes; Prior Academic Preparation Is Also Important for High Grades

There are two obvious and interrelated reasons why students may not do well in their courses—either they are not prepared for the academic work required by their high school courses or they are not coming to class and expending sufficient effort to do the requisite work. If the first is the main reason for course failures, it indicates that we need greater focus on preparing students in elementary schools for the academic demands of high school. If the second is the larger contributor to failure, then the problem results from students' behavior in high school and may be influenced by high school conditions. Some behavioral issues also may be addressed with more attention to attendance in elementary schools and better development of extra-academic skills, such as abilities to communicate well, work with others, develop leadership, improve group behaviors, and resolve conflicts. But behavioral issues suggest a need for critically examining high school culture and organization to identify ways that will encourage student participation and engagement. For simplicity, we begin by comparing academic preparation as measured by test scores with student effort as measured by attendance. In subsequent analyses, we also include students' reports of studying behavior as a measure of effort.

Before comparing their relationships with course failure, it is important to note that elementary test scores and high school attendance rates are strongly related to each other. Students with high achievement in elementary school are less likely to have high rates of course absence than those entering with low achievement, as shown in Figure 12. While almost half the students with the highest elementary achievement miss less than one week of high school classes per semester, only 11 percent of students entering with low achievement miss less than one week. More than a quarter of students with very low achievement in elementary school miss one month or more of classes per semester.

**FIGURE 12**
**Absences by Incoming Achievement**

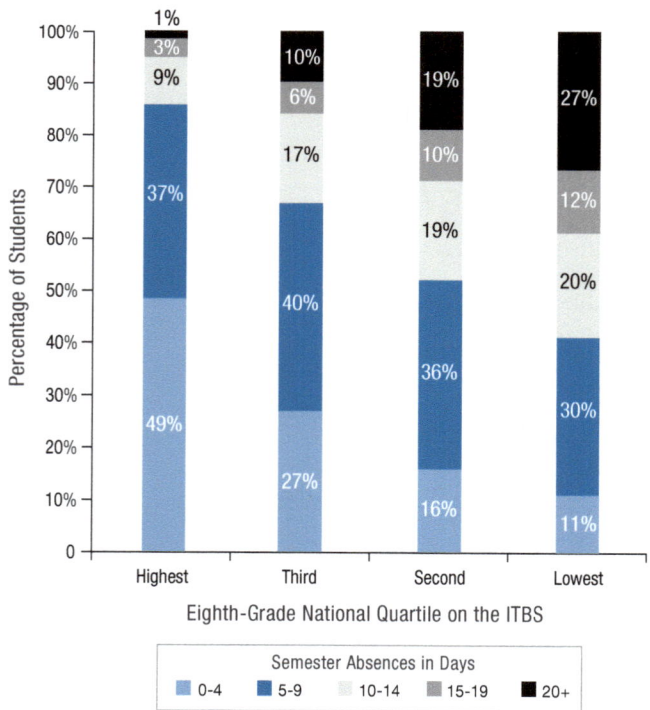

This relationship is not surprising; for some of these students, low achievement in elementary school probably resulted from high absence rates in elementary school. Also, there is likely a reciprocal relationship between achievement and absences, so that students who do not feel successful in their classes have less motivation to come to school. Still, given their low achievement, these are the students who most need to come to school, and they tend to attend the least often.

But it is not just students who enter high school with low achievement who are frequently absent. Attendance is a problem even among many high-achieving students. About half of the highest-achieving students—those entering high school with test scores in the top quartile nationally—missed more than one week of classes per semester, and almost three-fourths of students scoring in the third quartile (i.e., above national norms) missed more than one week per semester. Just one week of absence per semester indicates problems with students' grades.

Most people consider eighth-grade test scores to be good predictors of students' likelihood to do well in high school courses, and they are. However, course attendance is *eight times* more predictive of course failure in the freshman year than eighth-grade test scores; freshman absences can be used to predict 63 percent of the variation in course failures among freshmen in the 2004–05 entering class, while together math and reading eighth-grade ITBS scores predict only 8 percent of the variation in course failures. As shown in Figure 13, students who entered high school with very low eighth-grade achievement (with test scores that placed them in the bottom national quartile) who missed less than one week of classes per semester had fewer Fs, on average, than students entering high school with very high achievement (test scores in the top national quartile) who missed *one additional week* of classes (0.7 semester course failures, compared to 0.9). Likewise, students with the lowest eighth-grade test scores who missed just one week of classes averaged fewer Fs than students with the highest test scores who missed two weeks (1.3, compared to 2.1). As shown in Figure 13, students' failure rates increase dramatically with more course absences (across the horizontal axis), but rise only modestly as eighth-grade achievement

**FIGURE 13**

**Average Number of Fs by Absences and Eighth-Grade Test Scores**

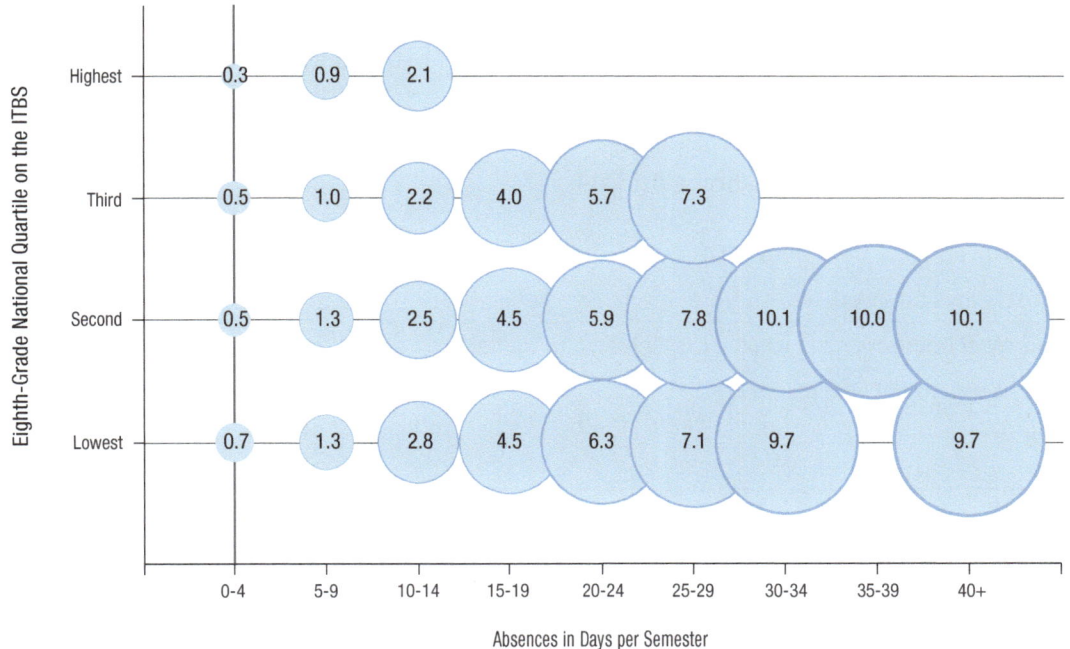

This figure only includes students still enrolled in school at the end of their freshman year. Only cells with at least 5 percent of students are included.

*How to read this chart:* The size of the circles indicates the extent of course failures. Students in the top row of the figure entered high school with the highest level of achievement, with test scores in the top national quartile. Very few of these students missed more than three weeks of school per semester, so there are no circles in columns that represent more than three weeks of course absences. However, students with high test scores who missed two weeks of classes in a semester averaged about two semester course failures in a year. High-achieving students who missed one week of classes per semester averaged one semester failure. Note that failure rates increase dramatically with greater absence (moving to the right along the horizontal axis). For example, failure rates are lower among students entering high school with the lowest test scores (in the bottom quartile) who missed less than a week of school than among students with the highest test scores (in the top quartile) who missed one week of school.

decreases (across the vertical axis). Among students with very high absence rates, incoming achievement is not at all predictive of failures. Just one week of absence is associated with a much greater likelihood of failure, regardless of incoming achievement.

There are likely a number of reasons that absences and failures are so strongly related. Obviously, attending class is a requirement for obtaining course credit and necessary for learning course material. In addition teachers' grading practices may incorporate absences or be affected by them. For example, teachers may reward good attendance through more lenient grading, while being especially strict in the grading of students who seem to be making less of an effort and are missing class. In addition, students who are performing poorly may least want to attend class. In many cases, there may be a downward spiral; missing class leads to poor performance, and poor performance leads students to avoid class. Research on dropping out has characterized the process as a gradual disengagement, where students miss more and more school, making it increasingly difficult to return.[1] Absences and failures may also be related for spurious reasons; for example, a poorly organized class may provide little motivation for student attendance and may also provide little support for learning. We are not saying that the relationship is completely causal, with absences determining course failures. But it does make sense that grades suffer if students are not in class to learn. The overwhelming strength of this relationship does suggest that failures are largely determined by course absence.

Among students with low absence rates, incoming achievement also predicts course failure. Students who entered high school with eighth-grade achievement

### How We Measured Students' Studying Behaviors

We created a measure of students' studying behaviors from four items on the CCSR survey of ninth- and tenth-graders, listed below. Together, the items formed a scale with a reliability of alpha=0.76. On average, 71 percent of students agreed or strongly agreed that they set aside time to do homework and study; 85 percent said they tried to do well on schoolwork even when it isn't interesting; 51 percent said they don't go out with friends if they need to study; while 44 percent said that they always study for tests.[A]

**How Much Do You Agree with the Following:**

| | Strongly Disagree | | | | Strongly Agree |
|---|---|---|---|---|---|
| • I set aside time to do my homework and study. | ☐ | ☐ | ☐ | ☐ | ☐ |
| • I try to do well on my schoolwork even when it isn't interesting to me. | ☐ | ☐ | ☐ | ☐ | ☐ |
| • If I need to study, I don't go out with my friends. | ☐ | ☐ | ☐ | ☐ | ☐ |
| • I always study for tests. | ☐ | ☐ | ☐ | ☐ | ☐ |

#### Sidebar Endnotes

**A** Another item that asked about the number of hours spent studying was initially included in the measure. However, it did not fit with the other items and lowered the reliability. We were concerned about including it in the measure because the number of hours that students studied was confounded with the degree to which they needed to study. While more time studying was associated with better outcomes when examined on its own, it was associated with worse outcomes once we controlled for other study habits. Thus, we chose not to include it as a control variable because it might be affected by the outcomes being studied.

---

in the bottom national quartile but missed less than one week of high school per semester were more than twice as likely to fail a course as students with similar absence rates but elementary achievement in the top national quartile (averaging 0.7 failures compared to 0.3 failures). Thus, academic preparation does matter, but students' behaviors in high school are more important.

Course attendance is also highly predictive of getting higher grades, not just avoiding failures. As with course failures, attendance is the strongest predictor of overall grades and of grades other than failures.[2] In fact, more than half of the students who miss less than one week of school per semester have a GPA of 3.0 (B average) or higher at the end of their first year, three-fourths have at least a 2.5 GPA, and 90 percent have at least a 2.0 GPA.[3] In other words, almost all students who have good attendance also have average or higher grades. However, while course failure is overwhelmingly associated with course attendance, academic preparation remains very important for getting higher grades. Without controlling for other student characteristics or behaviors, 17 percent of the student-to-student variability in GPAs can be explained by incoming test scores, while incoming test scores are associated with just 8 percent of the variability in course failures.

Looking beyond attendance, another measure of effort—students' self-reported study behaviors—is also predictive of freshman-year failures, and is particularly predictive of overall grades. Students who report high rates of studying earn GPAs that are 0.24 points higher, on average, than students who report low rates of studying, controlling for other background characteristics, including eighth-grade achievement and high school attendance.[4] Students who report high rates of studying also fail about 0.4 fewer courses than students with similar test scores and attendance who study little.[5]

## Course Grades Are Lower Among Boys and Nonwhite Students Than We Would Expect, Based on Their Behaviors and Academic Backgrounds

A number of student demographic characteristics are associated with course failure rates and GPA, such as race, gender, number of school moves prior to high school, economic status, and age at entry into high school. For example, boys, highly mobile students, and students entering older than age 14 are more likely to fail courses than other students. However, many of these relationships exist because students with these characteristics are more likely to have low elementary achievement, high absence rates, or both. Once we account for incoming achievement and course absences, the relationships of economic status, mobility, and age with GPA and failure largely disappear. (Tables 8 and 10 in Appendix D provide details on the relationships of these background variables using statistical models.

Gender and race, however, are still related to course failure and GPA, after controlling for incoming achievement and attendance. Gender is particularly predictive of failures and grades, with relationships that are similar in magnitude to those of incoming test scores. Without considering absence rates, boys receive one semester course failure more, on average, than girls in the same high school who have similar backgrounds and eighth-grade achievement. Boys' GPAs are also 0.4 points lower.[6] These differences are only partially explained by gender differences in attendance or studying. Boys and girls differ only slightly in their attendance and study rates, so when we control for these factors the gender difference in GPA declines by only 21 percent, and the difference in failure rates declines by only one-third. Given what we know about students' backgrounds and behaviors in high school, we still cannot explain the large gender gaps in GPAs and failure rates. The sidebar "Gender Differences in Course Performance" at the end of this chapter provides further details.

There are few differences in grades by race/ethnicity among students with similar academic and economic backgrounds unless we control for attendance and studying behaviors. Among students with similar academic and socioeconomic backgrounds, African-American students' GPAs are 0.2 points lower than the GPAs of white students, Latino students' GPAs are 0.1 points lower than whites, and Asian students' GPAs are 0.35 points higher than whites, on average. The only significant racial/ethnic difference in failure rates is that Asian students have 0.6 fewer semester course failures than other students, on average. Once we adjust for differences in absences and studying behaviors, however, racial/ethnic differences in grades and failure *increase*. When we compare students with similar absence and studying rates, nonwhite students, including Asian students, average about 0.4 more course failures than similar white students. Likewise, differences in GPAs between white students and both African-American and Latino students grow larger once we take attendance and studying into account. Only the difference in grades between Asian and other students is mostly explained—this difference shrinks by over two-thirds once we take into account attendance and studying. Academic behaviors explain the better performance of Asian students, but the lower GPAs of African-American and Latino students cannot be attributed to worse attendance and less studying. African-American and Latino ninth-grade students are getting lower grades than white students who have the same eighth-grade test scores, high school attendance, and study behaviors.

## Students' Background Characteristics Prior to High School Are Much Less Important in Explaining Failures Than Are Their Behaviors in High School

While a number of background characteristics predict freshman-year failure, the relationships are minute compared to those of attendance with failure. Students' background characteristics explain 7 percent of the differences in failure rates among students, and test scores explain an additional 5 percent (12 percent total), but absences and studying explain an additional 61 percent beyond test scores and demographic characteristics (73 percent total). See Appendix D for details.[7] Students' experiences and behavior while in high school are of utmost importance for passing courses; the focus of efforts to address failure should be on students' behaviors while in high school.[8]

Students' demographic characteristics and their previous test scores explain more of the variation in students' grades than in failure rates—31 percent. Absences and self-reported study behaviors are slightly more important, explaining an additional 34 percent of the variation in grades beyond test scores and demographic characteristics (64 percent total).[9] There seems to be a hierarchy: attendance is the most crucial factor for passing classes; however, to get high grades students need good attendance, effort, and good preparation. The extremely strong relationship that attendance holds with grades and failures suggests that we need to understand the factors behind course absences if we are going to improve students' grades and pass rates.

## Student Background Characteristics Largely Do Not Explain Differences in Absence Rates Among Students

Course absences are a serious problem in CPS, and these high absence rates underlie many of the problems with course failure and low GPAs. Attendance is affected by many factors that exist outside the high school, such as health, family stability, and students' experiences in elementary school. CPS predominantly serves low-income students who often experience more health problems than higher-income students, which interferes with attendance.[10] Yet, we can explain only a small amount of the differences across students' freshman year absence rates by their personal demographic and economic characteristics.

Background characteristics that have some association with absences include students' race, gender, poverty level, mobility in elementary school, eighth-grade test scores, and age at entry to high school. The strongest relationships are with eighth-grade test scores, elementary school mobility, and age at entry to high school.[11] As shown in the earlier chapter, students entering with high achievement are least likely to be absent more than two weeks per semester, while almost half the students entering high school with very low achievement are absent this often. Keeping constant other background characteristics (e.g., age, race, and gender), students with very low achievement before high school average five more days of absence per semester in their freshman year than students with very high achievement.[12] This suggests that we should incorporate attendance strategies as part of ninth-grade transition programs for low-achieving students.

Not surprisingly, highly mobile elementary school students also are likely to have more absences in high school, as are students who entered high school after age 14. For example, students who changed schools three or more times in their last three years of elementary school average six more days of absence per semester in high school than students with stable enrollment. These students are likely experiencing family and residential instability that affects their attendance. Students who began high school older than age 14 are absent 5 days more, on average, than students who entered at age 14 or younger, controlling for their test scores. Most students entering high school older than age 14 have been held back in grade at some point. Students entering high school who are old for their grade may be more likely to have a history of absence.[13] In addition, there is evidence that grade retention makes students more likely to withdraw from school, and so retention itself may bring on higher absence rates.[14]

Once elementary test scores, elementary mobility, and age on entering high school are taken into account, there are only very modest differences in absence rates by gender, race, or socioeconomic status. Controlling for other background characteristics, boys average just one more day of absence than girls. Asian students are absent three fewer days, on average, than African-American and white students with similar elementary test scores, mobility, and age. Latino students are absent about one fewer day than similar African-American and white students. Likewise, poverty shows only a small relationship with absence (once test scores, mobility, and age are controlled), with students from high-poverty neighborhoods absent 1.5 days more, on average, than students from low-poverty neighborhoods.[15] Even though they are significantly related to absence, all these individual student characteristics together explain less than one-fifth of the total variation in absence rates.[16] For the most part, demographic and academic background characteristics do not explain the large differences in absence rates among students.

## Gender Differences in Course Performance

The gender gap is one of the most pressing and least understood problems in high school reform today. It is a relatively new phenomenon, as graduation rates of girls nationwide did not surpass those of males until the early 1980s (CPS, 2000). Nationally, 65 percent of male students graduate, compared to 72 percent of female students.[A] In CPS, only 39 percent of African-American boys and 51 percent of Latino boys graduate,[B] and those boys who graduate tend to have very low GPAs.[C] Among CPS freshmen, boys are more likely than girls to have very low GPAs, and they are much less likely to have high GPAs (see Figure 14). Only 5 percent of first-time freshman boys in CPS had GPAs of 3.5 or higher in the 2005–06 school year, while almost 30 percent had GPAs of 1.0 or lower.

While there is growing research identifying the gender gap, there is little that helps to explain it. There is some research suggesting that behaviors such as self-discipline may underlie part of the gender gap.[D] In Chicago, it is true that boys have somewhat higher absence rates than girls and report slightly lower rates of studying.[E] However, these differences explain only one-third of the differences in grades between girls and boys in CPS. Among students who attend the same high school and have the same attendance, study habits, and eighth-grade test scores, boys' GPAs are 0.3 points lower on average than girls', and their failure rates are higher by 0.6 Fs.[F] Other research has shown that students tend to perform better when their teachers are the same gender, suggesting that the over-representation of female teachers may underlie some of the differences.[G] However, the performance differences that can be attributed to teacher-student match are quite modest. These teacher-gender effects do very little to explain the sizable gaps in performance, although they do lead us to wonder what it is about same-gender teachers that may facilitate learning (e.g., better understanding of behavioral cues).

In the popular press, a number of potential explanations have been posed for the gender gap,

**FIGURE 14**

Distribution of Freshman GPAs by Gender for Students Entering CPS High Schools in 2005-06

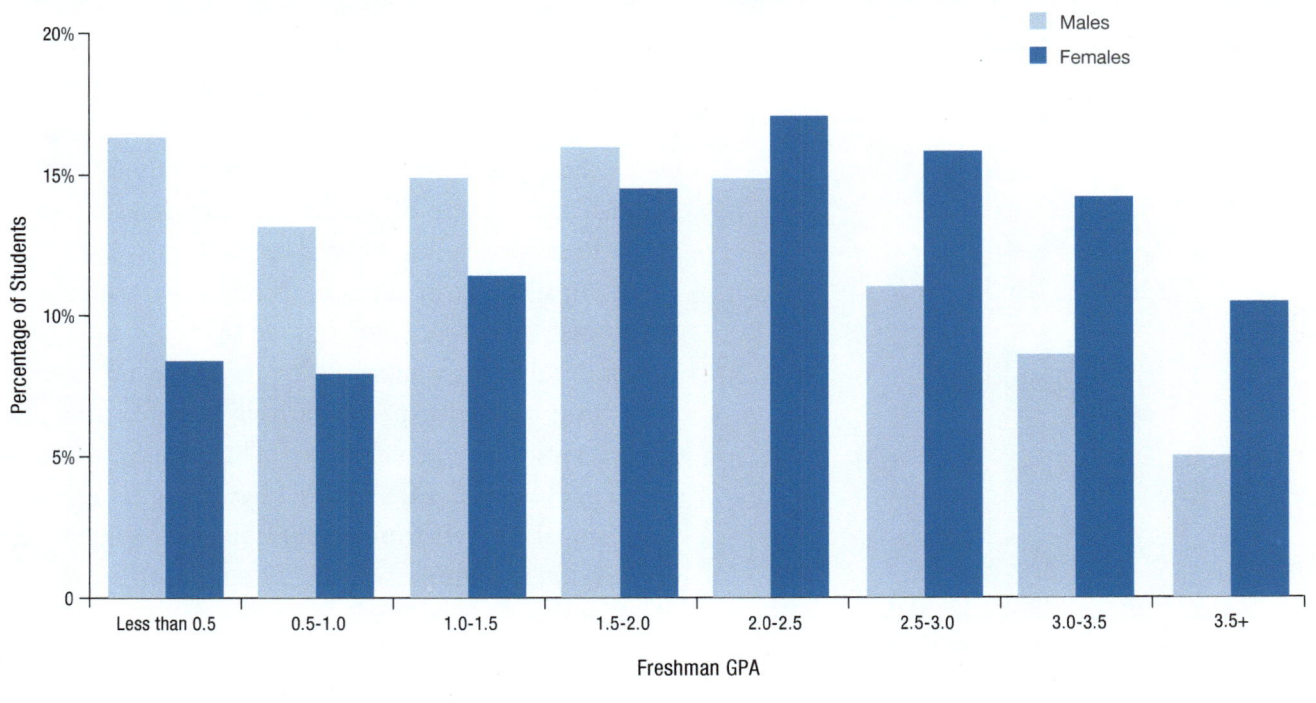

Chapter 2 | 21

including biological differences, inappropriate behavioral expectations for boys, and curricula that are too focused on topics of interest to girls.[H] In addition, cultural expectations have been proposed to explain the particularly low graduation rates of minority males.[I] However, there is little data to support these explanations, and several do not hold up when we examine Chicago data. Concerns about the curricula tend to point to English classes as less appealing to boys; yet in Chicago, the gender gap is not markedly different across subjects (see Figure 15). Cultural explanations seem unlikely, given that the gender gap is not confined to specific racial/ethnic groups but exists across all racial/ethnic breakdowns.[J]

To try to better understand what might underlie the gender gap in CPS, we looked to see whether there were differences in the size of the gender gap across high schools and whether these differences were related to the climate in the school. In all CPS high schools, boys perform more poorly in their classes, on average, than girls; but there are differences across schools in the size of the gender gap.[K] Schools that attract high-achieving students have smaller gender gaps in course failures, but this is because course failures are less common in these schools. There are equally large gender gaps in GPAs, regardless of the academic or economic composition of the school. *However, differences in failure rates by gender are smaller in schools where more students report strong student-teacher trust, personal support from teachers, schoolwide press to prepare for the future, and peer support for academic achievement.*[L] Each of these factors is also related to lower schoolwide failure rates, but they may be particularly crucial for boys at risk of failure. Only one measure of school climate is associated with a smaller gender gap in overall GPA: the degree to which teachers report individualizing instruction.[M] Boys' GPAs are not as far behind girls' GPAs in schools in which more teachers reported adjusting their pacing and strategies in response to students' understanding.

These relationships are highly suggestive that classroom conditions play a role in the gender gap. They suggest to us that boys at risk of failure may be particularly sensitive to the degree to which teachers reach out to provide academic support and tailor instruction. In addition, there are systematic ways in which boys view the climate in their school differently than girls. Boys tend to report much lower levels of teacher personal support than girls, as well as peer support, for academics (see Figure 16). The difference in boys' perceptions of their peers' support for academics may indicate different norms of academic behavior for boys—differences that may be read by teachers as lower levels of engagement or interest. While purely speculative at this point, we could imagine that boys might have greater difficulty approaching teachers when they are having problems, particularly if they feel that their peers would not be supportive of help-seeking behavior. The substantial difference in boys' and girls' reports of personal support from teachers likewise suggests that boys are receiving less academic support from teachers than they feel that they need.

**FIGURE 15**

**Gender Differences in Course Performance by Subject**

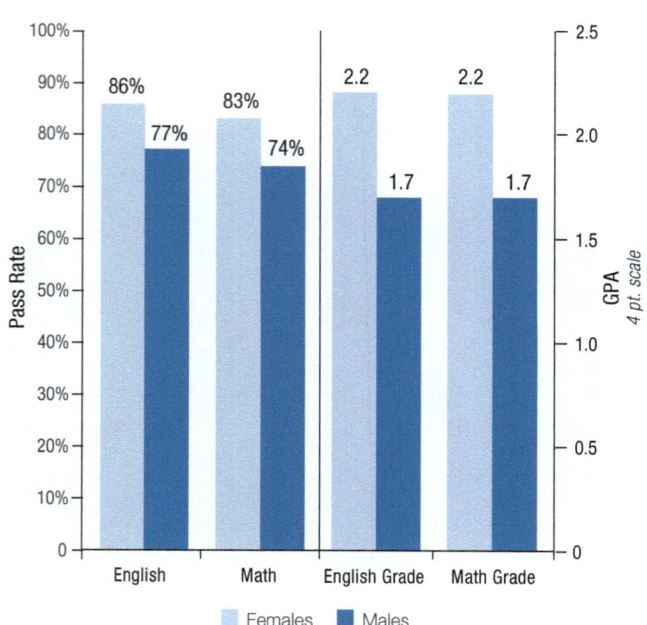

## FIGURE 16

**Differences Between Girls' and Boys' Reports of School Climate**

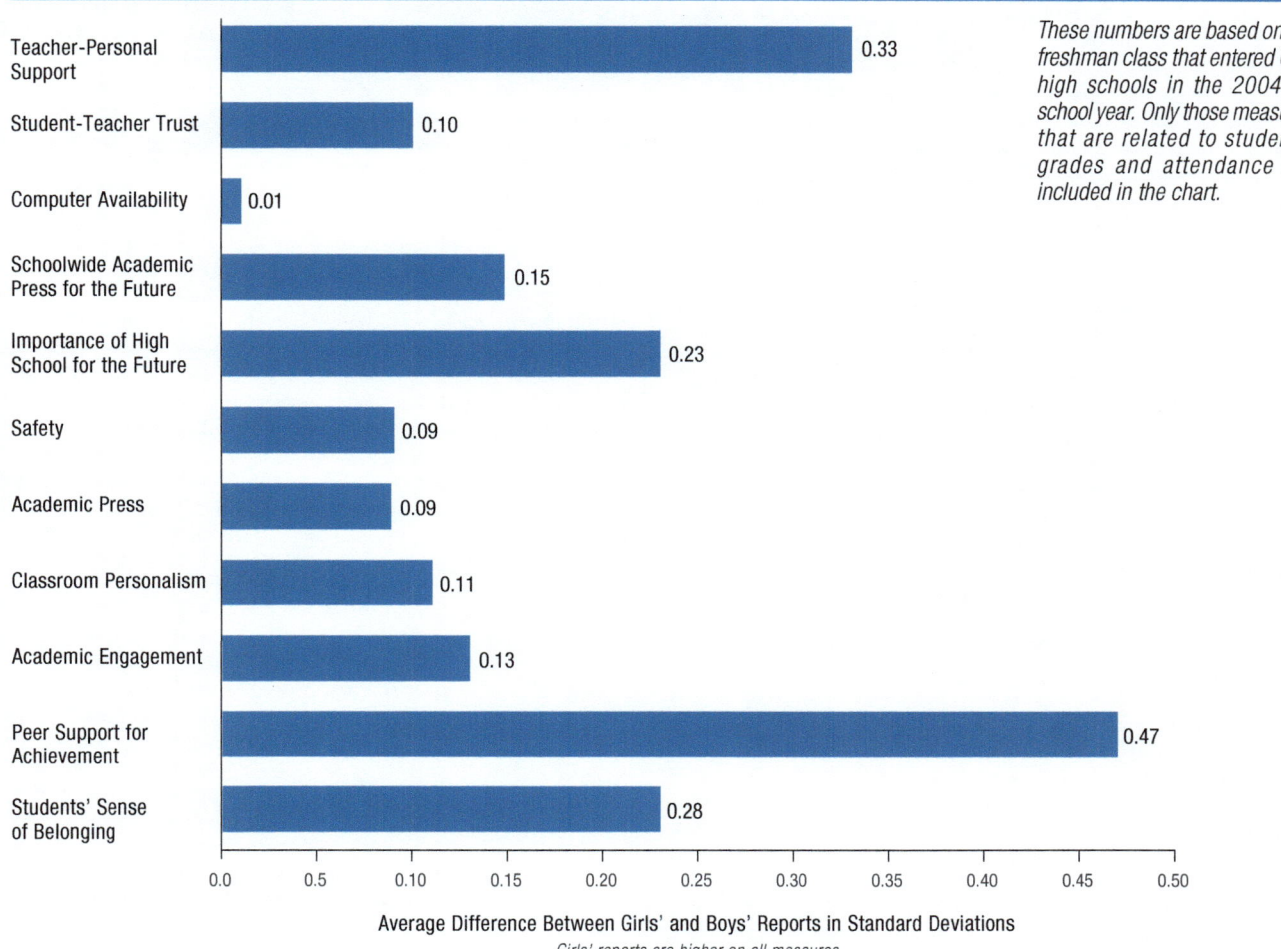

*These numbers are based on the freshman class that entered CPS high schools in the 2004-05 school year. Only those measures that are related to students' grades and attendance are included in the chart.*

Average Difference Between Girls' and Boys' Reports in Standard Deviations
*Girls' reports are higher on all measures*

## Sidebar Endnotes

A   Greene and Winters (2006).
B   Allensworth (2005).
C   Roderick, Nagaoka, and Allensworth (2006).
D   Duckworth and Seligman (2006).
E   Boys are absent 1.3 more days than girls, on average, in their first year of high school. Forty-eight percent of first-year freshman boys report studying or doing homework for less than two hours per week, compared to 44 percent of girls; 7 percent of boys report spending ten or more hours per week on studying/homework, compared to 9 percent of girls.
F   These differences can be seen in Table 8 (Fs) and Table 10 (GPA) in Appendix D.
G   Dee (2005).
H   Brooks (2006); Leving and Sacks (2006); and Tyre (2006).
I   Patterson (2006).
J   National data reported by Greene and Winters (2006) show that the gender gap in graduation rates is largest among minority students. However, these comparisons are based on percentage point differences rather than ratios. If comparisons are made in terms of the ratio of male to female nongraduates, the differences between racial/ethnic groups in the gender gap become minimal. Using Greene and Winters' figures, across all ethnic groups but Asians, the percentage of nongraduates is about 25 percent higher among males than among females (among Asians the male rate is 11 percent higher). In CPS, the percentage of nongraduates is about 30 percent higher among males than among females across all racial/ethnic groups but Asians (where the rate is 64 percent higher).
K   Gender gaps were studied through two-level hierarchical linear models with variables for student backgrounds and elementary achievement entered at level 1, similar to those shown in Appendix C. However, these models allowed the gender coefficient to vary by school.
L   Residuals of the gender gap coefficient from the models predicting course failures were correlated with measures of school climate at the following levels: school-level academic press for the future (-0.35), student-teacher trust (-0.35), teacher concrete support (-0.28), and peer academic support (-0.27).
M   Teacher individualization of instruction was correlated with the GPA gender gap coefficient at r=0.22.

## Chapter 2 Endnotes

1 Alexander, Entwisle, and Kabbani (2001); Bridgeland, DiIulio, and Morison (2006).

2 The analyses presented here use students' overall GPA. The same analyses were performed using students' GPA in their passed courses, but the results were similar and so overall GPA is presented here for simplicity.

3 These statistics remain constant across different cohorts of first-time freshman, including those who started high school in fall 2000 and those who started fall 2004.

4 This is a difference of two standard deviations (see Table 10 in Appendix D).

5 This is a difference of two standard deviations (see Table 8 in Appendix D).

6 These numbers control for eighth-grade test scores, poverty in students' neighborhoods, socioeconomic status of students' neighborhoods, mobility in elementary school, age at entry to high school, and two school characteristics: academic and socioeconomic composition of the student body.

7 These figures are out of the total variance (at both the individual and school levels).

8 There are likely unmeasured factors that affect students' course attendance in high school, unrelated to their school experiences, such as family instability. However, it is also likely that these factors would be highly correlated with students' background characteristics, such as socioeconomic status, mobility, age, and elementary school test scores, and thus also controlled to some extent in the models.

9 The strong relationship between grades and absence is not simply an artifact of the very lowest-achieving students having extremely high absence rates. The relationship remains about as strong as if we predict nonfailing grades, or if we use a transformed version of absence that reduces the influence of extreme cases.

10 Newacheck et al. (1998); and Starfield (1982).

11 See Table 6 in Appendix D for details.

12 High and low achievement is defined as one standard deviation above and below the mean.

13 Students who are held back in grade tend to have higher rates of absence pre-retention than students not held back (Alexander, Entwisle, and Dauber, 2003). This could be due to the relationship between absence and achievement, and also because teachers may use attendance as one criterion for promotion, along with achievement.

14 E.g., Grissom, and Shepard (1989); Roderick (1994); Allensworth (2005).

15 This is the difference in average absence rates between students whose neighborhood poverty level is one standard deviation below average, and those one standard deviation above average. These figures are calculated from a nested model that accounts for differences across schools—see Table 6 in Appendix D.

16 See Table 6 and Table 7 in Appendix D for details on the statistical models relating background characteristics to course attendance.

# Chapter 3

# What Matters for Grades, Failure, and Attendance: School Practices

Grades and course failures are strongly tied to student behaviors in high school, particularly course attendance. Only a small portion of students' attendance patterns can be explained by their background characteristics prior to high school. Given this, what other factors are related to attendance? One answer is in students' experiences in high school.

In this chapter, we look for differences among schools in students' attendance, grades, and course failures that cannot be explained by the characteristics that students bring with them prior to high school. We begin by looking simply at the degree to which there is variation in attendance and grades among students with similar backgrounds at different schools. Following this, we show that particular school practices and climates are related to better outcomes among schools that serve similar types of students. This analysis is limited to looking at effects averaged across classrooms and students within each school. We know that individual students' experiences vary widely within schools, and there is substantially more variation in attendance rates and course grades among students within the same school than there is across schools. However, our measurement system does not allow us to look more closely than the school level.[1] This work provides initial evidence that school climate and practices matter.

## Course Attendance Varies Substantially Across Schools That Serve Similar Types of Students

There is substantial variation from one school to another in attendance rates, even when we compare students with similar eighth-grade achievement and background characteristics. After removing differences in absence rates that can be explained by students' backgrounds and prior achievement, absence rates vary across schools by about 6.5 days per semester. When we confine the comparison to schools serving similar types of students, absence rates vary by about 4.4 days per semester.[2] This is about a week of absence per semester (almost two weeks per year) that cannot be accounted for by students' backgrounds or the composition of students in their school.

Of course, student absence is caused by illness, doctor appointments, personal or family problems, extended vacations, weather, transportation difficulties, or the need to work. Our evidence, however, suggests that the need to work is not a primary cause of absence, and that schools can influence the degree to which students miss class. Only 10 percent of first-year CPS freshmen work more than ten hours per week, and work may indeed interfere with the attendance of these students.[3] But for the 69 percent of students who do not work at all and the 21 percent who work less than ten hours per week, work is not contributing to absence. Likewise, if sickness, personal/family issues, or transportation problems were alone responsible for student absence, we would expect absence rates to be similar across the school year. However, our data show that freshman attendance, which is bad enough in fall semester, is even worse in spring semester. In some schools freshmen miss an additional week or more of classes in spring semester than they do in fall semester, while in other schools absence rates are similar in both terms; this suggests that school effects are driving absence, along with personal reasons. There are also substantial differences in absence rates across schools, suggesting school effects on attendance.

Figure 17 shows the wide variation in absence rates across schools for students with similar incoming achievement, with details provided in Table 2 (see Appendix A). One trend that is striking in Figure 17 is the strong relationship between school absence rates and the degree to which the school enrolls high- or low-achieving students. Two students with similar incoming achievement are likely to have very different absence rates based on the average incoming achievement of other students at their school. Students who attend schools with high average achievement tend to have better attendance rates than similar students attending schools with low average achievement. This is partly because students who attend schools with higher average achievement than their own probably have other characteristics that are also associated with better absence rates (e.g., highly educated parents and fewer disciplinary problems).[4] However, the effects of academic composition seem to be more than the sum of individual characteristics of students. Student composition affects the climate of the school (see the sidebar "Many Aspects of School Climate Are Closely Tied to Student Body Composition"). One can imagine that it is easier to develop intervention plans for individual students when only a few students are doing poorly, while it may be difficult to convince students that they need to attend more often when frequent absence is common.

The strong relationship between academic composition and absence rates highlights the difficulty of improving a school with a large percentage of low-achieving students. Letgers and Balfanz (2004) have shown that a large percentage of dropouts in this country are enrolled in "dropout factories." In these schools, which serve predominantly low-income students, freshmen vastly outnumber seniors due to low rates of promotion, and school staff members are overwhelmed by the concentration of student needs. They found poverty to be the main correlate of weak promotion rates.[5] While we found academic composition to be more predictive of absences than school poverty, the tight relationship between poverty and academic composition may make the root cause immaterial in terms of policy. Schools serving large proportions of students who have not been successful in elementary school face substantially more challenges than schools receiving mostly high-achieving students.

# FIGURE 17
**Freshman-Year Absence Rates by School by Students' Eighth-Grade Achievement**

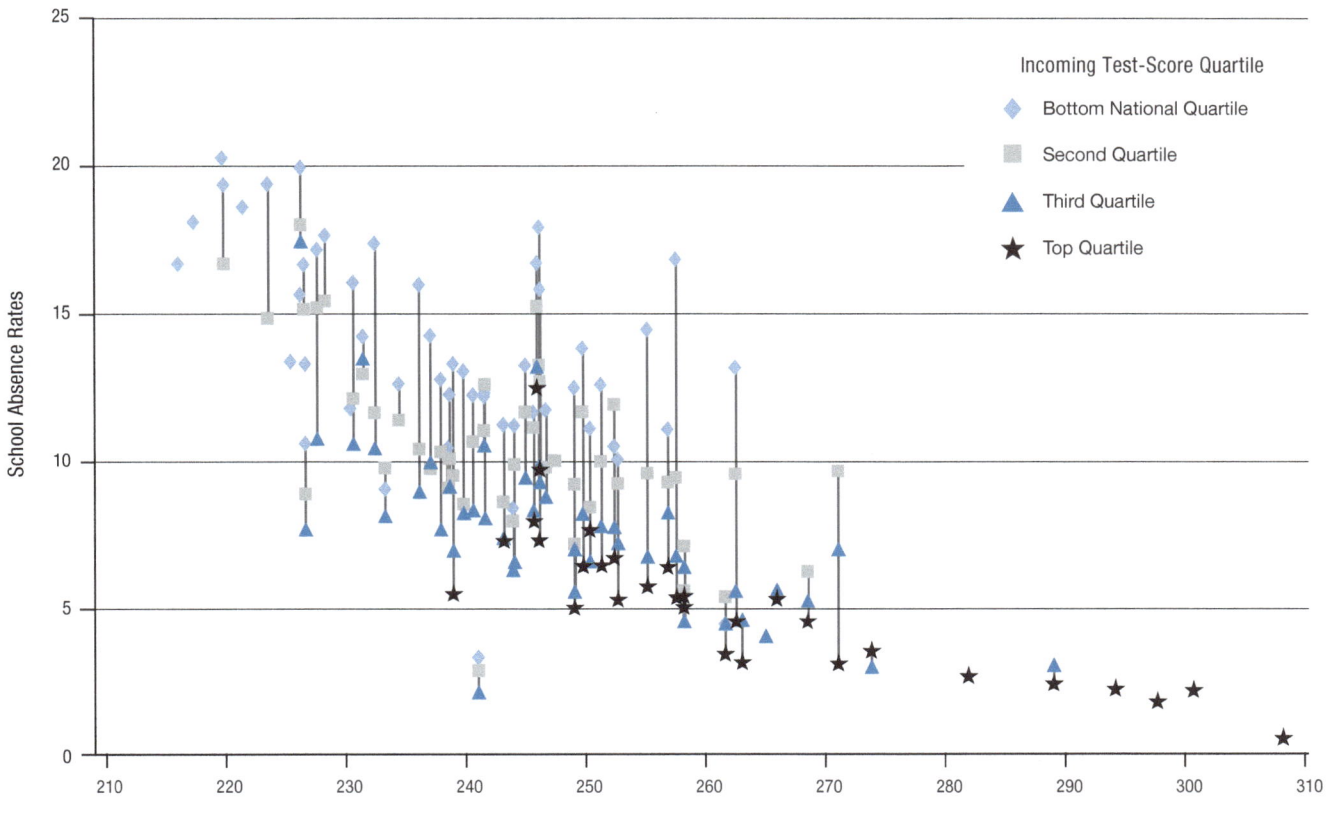

*How to read this figure: Each dot shows absence rates for students in a specific school entering high school with a specific achievement level. A school could be represented by as many as four symbols, each representing students with different incoming test scores. Symbols representing the same school are connected by a line. The different symbols allow for a comparison of students with similar eighth-grade achievement. Diamonds show absence rates for students entering high school with elementary test scores that put them in the bottom national quartile. Squares represent absence rates for students entering high school with test scores in the second-to-lowest national quartile. Many of the lowest-achieving schools in the system only enroll students with achievement that is below norms, and for this reason the far left side of the figure mostly has diamonds and squares. Triangles represent absence rates among students in the third national quartile, while stars represent students in the top national quartile. On the far right side of the chart are the selective enrollment schools. These schools only enroll students with test scores above national norms, and so they are only represented with triangles (for those students in the third quartile) and stars (for those students in the top quartile). By comparing similar symbols, the chart shows that students with similar incoming achievement have very different absence rates at different schools.*

*Consider an exceptional school — North-Grand. The average incoming math ITBS score for students entering North-Grand in 2004 was 241 standard score points, and you can easily identify the symbols representing North-Grand by looking for the lowest set of symbols at 241 on the horizontal axis. These symbols are far below the cluster of symbols representing other schools because absent rates are much lower than typical at this school. Average absence rates for North-Grand students are under a week per semester, even among those with eighth-grade test scores place them in the bottom national quartile (the diamond). In comparison, at other schools serving similar students, students entering high school with test scores in the bottom quartile (the diamonds) tend to have absence rates between 8 and 18 days per semester. North-Grand is also different from a number of other schools in the degree to which the symbols are close together. At North-Grand, absence rates are similar across students with very different incoming test scores (represented by different symbols). At many schools, students with high eighth-grade test scores have much lower absence rates than students with low eighth-grade test scores; in these other schools the symbols are spread apart.*

Still, while academic composition is strongly related to absence, schools with the same academic composition often have very different absence rates. This can be seen in Figure 17 by comparing similar symbols (representing students with similar academic backgrounds) that have a similar location on the horizontal axis. For example, at schools with typical incoming achievement (between 240 and 250 standard score points), absence rates among students in the second achievement quartile (represented by square symbols) vary from less than 5 days per semester at one school to 15 days at another.

There are also substantial differences across schools in the degree to which students' incoming achievement is related to course absences. Some schools show large differences in absence rates by students' elementary achievement, while others show only small differences across students with varying levels of incoming achievement. The relationship between academic preparation and attendance depends on the school that a student attends—at some schools incoming achievement matters substantially, but at other schools it does not.[6] Policies and practices of schools likely moderate the relationship between academic background and course performance.

## Grades and Failure Rates Also Vary Across Schools, But School Differences in Grades Are Small Compared to the Effects of Academic Preparation

Among students with similar background characteristics and eighth-grade test scores, average failure rates differ by about 1.4 Fs across schools.[7] In other words, two students who look alike in terms of their race, gender, socioeconomic background, elementary school mobility, age, and eighth-grade test scores coming into high school may have failure rates that are different by 1.4 Fs, based solely on which school they attend. These differences are modestly related to the composition of students in the school. Controlling for the average achievement level of students entering the school and average poverty level, failure rates among students with similar backgrounds vary across schools by about 1.4 Fs.

GPAs vary by about 0.3 points across schools, after controlling for students' incoming achievement and background, and for the composition of students in the school.[8] A difference of 0.3 grade points sounds small, but it is not trivial—such a difference could have a sizable effect on a student's eligibility for college. To achieve an increase of 0.3 points in GPA would require a student with straight Cs to receive Bs in 5 out of 14 semester classes—not a small feat. Furthermore, a few schools have particularly high or low GPAs, given the students they serve. We should better understand why these differences exist and how they may be affected by different practices or standards. However, it is important to note that the differences between schools in average grades are modest. This occurs, in part, because academic preparation is an important factor behind getting high grades at all schools.

The between-school variation in grades looks different than the variation in attendance because grades are more dependent on students' incoming academic skills. Figure 18 graphs average GPAs by school for students with different levels of eighth-grade achievement (see Table 2 in Appendix A for details). This chart is similar to Figure 17, which graphed absences; however, the picture is quite different. Unlike Figure 17, there are fairly distinct ranges of GPAs across all schools among students with similar pre–high school achievement. For example, students entering high school with achievement in the third national quartile tend to have GPAs between 1.8 and 2.5 at almost all schools, while those entering with scores in the second quartile tend to have GPAs between 1.5 and 2.0—note that there is variation within each achievement quartile in average grades, but only a slight overlap across achievement quartiles. While there are differences across schools in average grades, and at a few schools these differences are sizable, in general, school effects are small compared to the effects of academic preparation.

There is a common perception that students receive high grades in low-performing schools because of low academic standards. Because grades are seen as subjective, they are often considered unreliable as indicators of academic achievement. The patterns shown in Figure 18 contradict this perception—poorly prepared students are unlikely to get good grades just

**FIGURE 18**
**Freshman Year GPA by School by Students' Eighth-Grade Achievement**

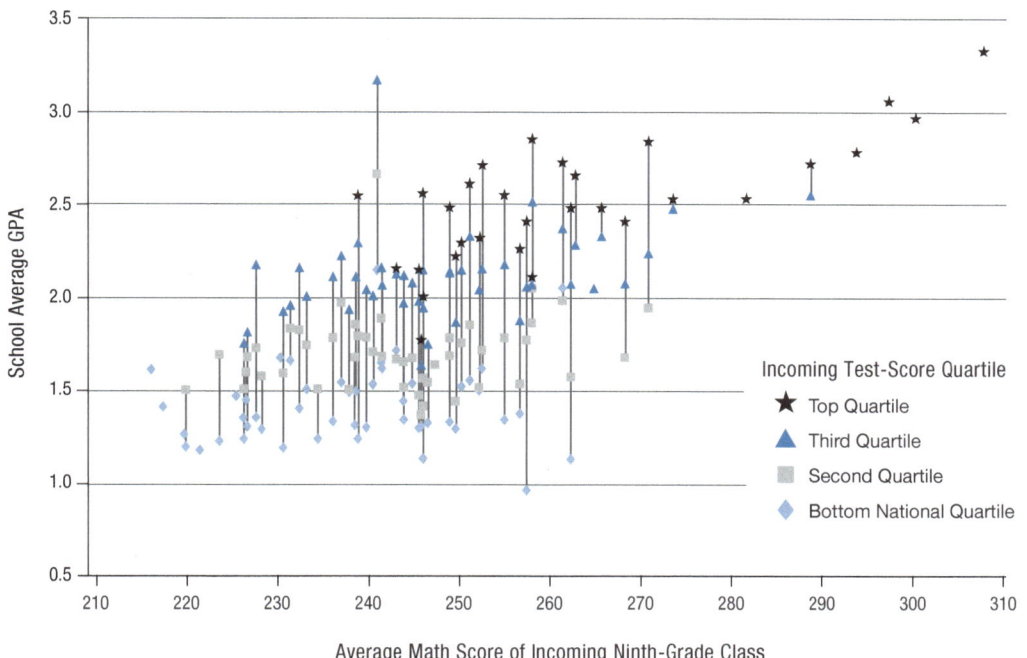

## Many Aspects of School Climate Are Closely Tied to the Student Body Composition

The analyses presented in this report look at the relationships of school climate with student outcomes after taking out any effects that might be attributable to the types of students served by the school. Many aspects of climate are related to schools' academic and socioeconomic composition, and many of these same features are related to student outcomes. It can be difficult to disentangle these relationships. Table 5 (see Appendix C) shows the strength of some of these relationships, in particular for schools that enroll higher-achieving students. Those students are more likely to report a safer school environment, fewer disciplinary problems, and better peer behavior in class; those students are more likely to report that they feel like they belong; and those teachers are more likely to expect students to go to college, and to report productive relationships with parents and high levels of commitment to the school.

It becomes difficult to disentangle the extent to which these features of school climate themselves affect student outcomes. Student outcomes are better than expected in schools with high-achieving students and positive school climates. It might just be that having many high-achieving students together in the same school improves each individual student's achievement and also simultaneously improves the climate. Alternatively, student body composition might affect the climate of the school, which in turn affects student outcomes.

Because we cannot tell the extent to which each is true, we only show the relationships with climate that remain after we have removed the effects of student body composition on student outcomes. This may be overly conservative, in that some features of schools may not be found significant because they are so strongly related to student body composition that their effects cannot be disentangled. However, this analysis provides comparisons among similar schools, showing why schools that serve similar types of students have different student outcomes.

because they attend a low-performing school. One might think that a school that only enrolls poorly prepared students (e.g., only students with test scores below national norms) would give As and Bs to the best of those students. Yet, that is not the case—few students who enroll in these schools receive As and Bs. Undoubtedly, there are somewhat different standards for grades across teachers and schools. In fact, statistical models show that students with the same number of absences tend to have slightly higher GPAs at schools where absence is common.[9] However, standards are not so much lower that they compensate for the very different levels of preparation and attendance at the different types of schools.

While concern is often voiced that standards are set too low in CPS, Figure 18 suggests the opposite—few students in CPS receive high grades at any school. At only a few selective-enrollment schools are average GPAs higher than 2.5 (C+). Even students who enter high school with elementary achievement in the top national quartile are unlikely to achieve a B average at all but the top few high schools in the city. Why students receive such poor grades is a topic that needs further exploration—are there too many competing demands or stressors on students, are standards set too high, is instruction weak or poorly organized, or are expectations for performance set too low? We begin to explore these questions by looking at the characteristics of schools with GPAs, failures, and absence rates that are higher or lower than expected, given the students that they serve.

## Course Performance Is Better in Schools with Strong Teacher-Student Relationships and Where Students See High School as Relevant for Their Future

There are significant differences among schools in average grades, failure rates, and attendance, even after we take into account the backgrounds and incoming academic skills of students they serve. To better understand what school factors may affect student course performance, we look at a number of aspects of the learning climate in schools, measured with surveys of students and teachers in CPS conducted by the Consortium on Chicago School Research (CCSR).

Table 3 in Appendix B lists some of the specific concepts of climate and practices that we measured with a survey administered in spring 2005. These include a wide range of topics related to how students interact with each other, their parents, and their teachers; how strongly the school supports students and their plans for the future; and various aspects of interactions among teachers around instruction. These measures of school climate were compared to average school absences, failure rates, and GPA, after adjusting them for differences that would be expected simply based on the characteristics of students entering the high school, including individual background, entering achievement, and composition of the student body.[10] Table 4 in Appendix C provides the details, which we summarize here. In general, grades, failure, and absence rates were significantly better than expected, given the students served by the school, in schools characterized by two features—supportive relationships between teachers and students, and a perception among students that the work they were doing in high school was preparing them for the future.

In particular, student performance is better where students report high levels of trust for their teachers and where they report that teachers provide personal support to them. As shown in Figure 19, students at schools with high levels of trust between teachers and students averaged 2.3 fewer days of absence per semester (5 days per year) than similar students at similar schools where there was little trust between students and teachers. Students averaged 0.8 fewer Fs in schools with high levels of trust, compared to similar students in schools with low levels of trust (see Figure 20), while GPAs were 0.2 points higher (see Figure 21). This is consistent with other research that found that schools with strong teacher-student relationships are more likely to have greater student engagement, reduced absences, and better graduation rates.[11] Weak teacher-student relationships can make it difficult for teachers to adequately monitor and support students.[12] The importance of teacher-student personal relationships in affecting grades and attendance also shows up in the degree to which students report personalization in the classroom and personal

**FIGURE 19**

**Relationships of School Climate Measures with Course Absences**

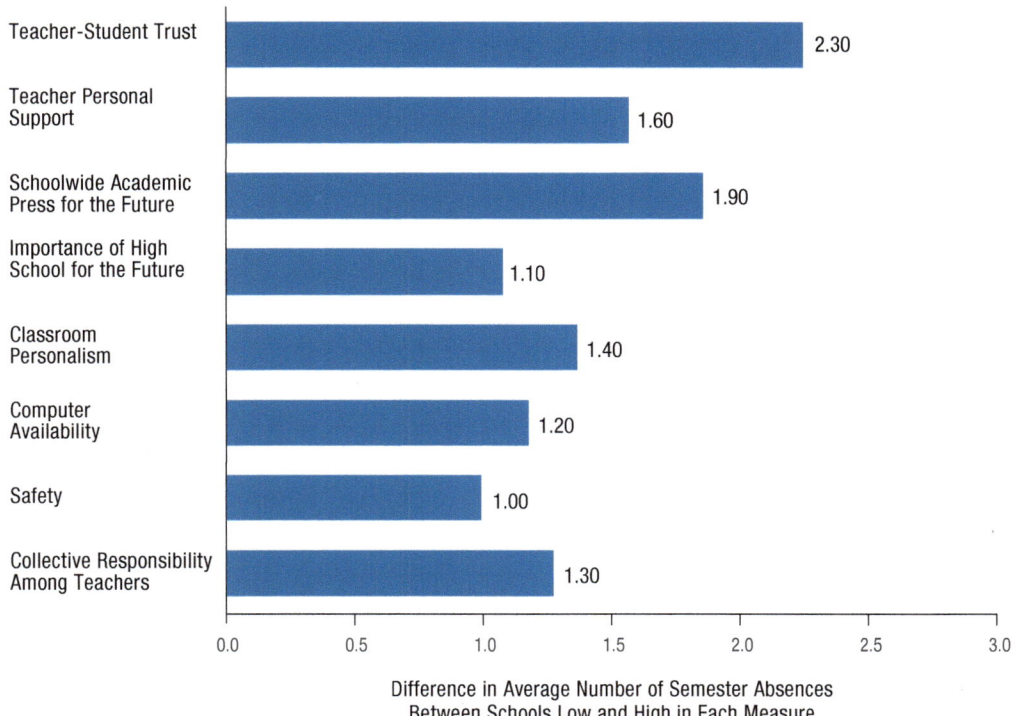

*These are relationships that remain after controlling for individual students' background characteristics (SES, gender, race, age at beginning high school, mobility in elementary school) and eighth-grade achievement test scores, as well as the composition of students in the school (average poverty level, and average incoming eighth-grade achievement). Schools that are high in measure are one standard deviation above average, those that are low are one standard deviation below average. See Table 3 in Appendix B for a list of all measures that were examined.*

**FIGURE 20**

**Relationships of School Climate Measures with Course Failures**

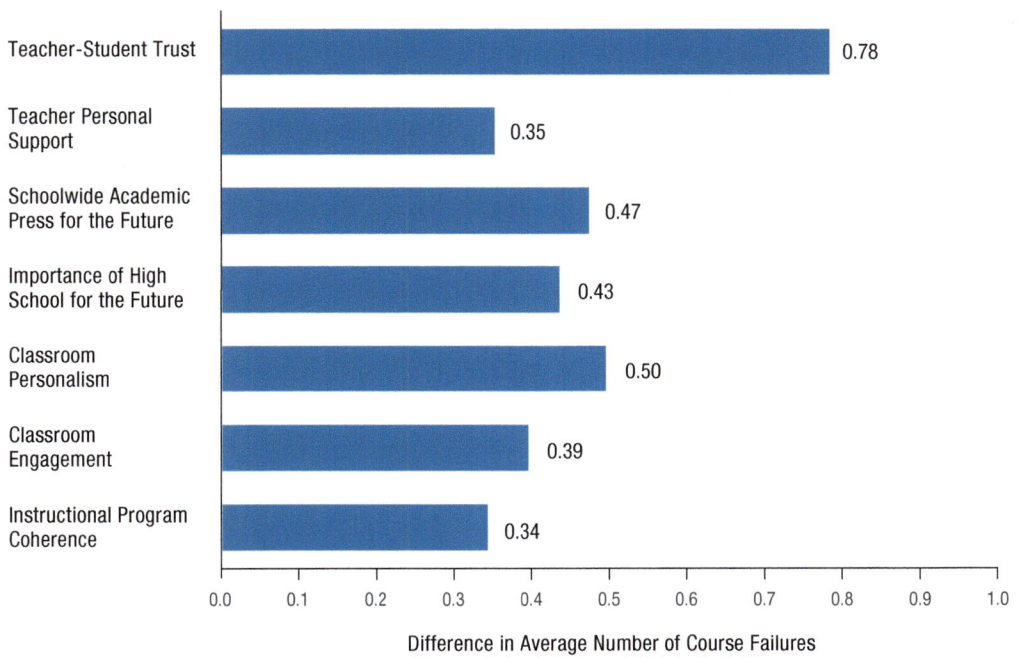

*These are relationships that remain after controlling for individual students' background characteristics (SES, gender, race, age at beginning high school, mobility in elementary school) and eighth-grade achievement test scores, as well as the composition of students in the school (average poverty level, and average incoming eighth-grade achievement). Schools that are high in measure are one standard deviation above average, those that are low are one standard deviation below average. See Table 3 in Appendix B for a list of all measures that were examined.*

Chapter 3

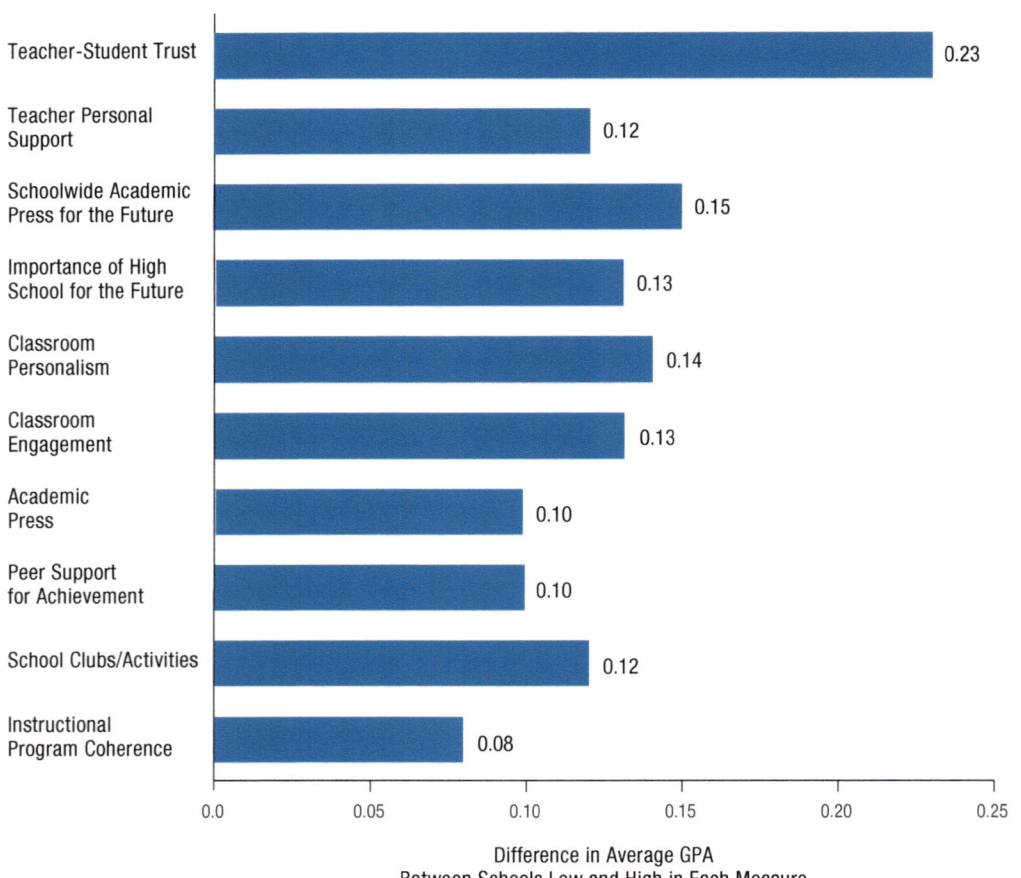

**FIGURE 21**

**Relationships of School Climate Measures with Average School GPA**

These are relationships that remain after controlling for individual students' background characteristics (SES, gender, race, age at beginning high school, mobility in elementary school) and eighth-grade achievement test scores, as well as the composition of students in the school (average poverty level, and average incoming eighth-grade achievement). Schools that are high in measure are one standard deviation above average, those that are low are one standard deviation below average. See Table 3 in Appendix B for a list of all measures that were examined.

support from teachers. Failure and absence rates were lower, and GPAs were higher, in schools where more students felt that their classroom teachers gave them individual attention and showed personal concern for them. Failure and absence rates were also better in schools with substantial personalization in classes compared to those with little personalization.

The strength of the relationship with classroom personalism is particularly noteworthy, given that it is measured at the school level with each student reporting on only one English or math class, rather than across all their classes. There are substantial differences across classrooms within the same school in the degree to which students report personalism. Therefore, we would expect the relationship of classroom personalism and engagement with attendance, grades, and failure to be even more pronounced across classrooms within a school than across schools.

Schools also differ in the general climate for learning that exists across classrooms towards the purpose of learning. Those schools that are able to make the connection between high school and students' futures tend to have lower absence and failure rates and higher average grades. These are schools in which more students report that what they do in high school matters for college and the workforce. Schools where many students felt that high school grades matter for success in college and the workforce and that classes give useful preparation for life averaged fewer absences and failures, and higher grades, than schools where few students felt high school was relevant for their future. Likewise, schools where students report that there is a schoolwide press for all students—not just the top students—to have high aspirations, work hard, and plan for the future tend to have lower failure rates than expected, given the types of students served by the school. In other words, failure rates are lower and grades are higher when school is seen as relevant and important for the future, and all students are pressed to prepare for life after high school. While relevance is measured at the school level in this work, it seems likely that perceptions of the relevance of school are tied to students' perceptions of their individual courses and the extent to which the work they do in those courses is meaningful. Researchers have shown that students produce higher-quality work when assignments have meaning to them.[13]

The two constructs that come out as most distinguishing schools in terms of students' course performance—the degree to which school is seen as relevant for the future and strong teacher-student relationships—are consistent with many of the current recommendations heard nationally on high school reform.[14] These recommendations have sometimes been conceptualized with a third component, rigor, as the three Rs—rigor, relevance, and relationships. We have only two measures of academic rigor available in this analysis—students' perceptions of academic press and teachers' reports of assignment demands. Neither shows a strong relationship with grades or failures, but we should not expect that rigorous coursework would necessarily translate into higher grades. Slow-paced work that is not challenging might lead to disengagement, but fast-paced and challenging work requires more effort from students.[15] Thus, rigorous work might have contradictory effects on grades, even if it leads to better academic skills. Still, it is notable that neither academic press nor rigorous academic demands is associated with higher rates of failure. In fact, grades are slightly higher than expected at schools where students report higher levels of academic press. These are schools where students report that teachers expect all students to participate and to achieve at high levels. In other words, students have higher grades in schools where more students report that their teachers challenge them with difficult work and questions.[16]

Relationships between teachers and students matter, as does the relevance of school. In addition, some resources at the school seem to matter for attendance, grades, and failure rates. Attendance was better than expected at schools where students reported access to computing technology at school. Schools in which many students participate in extracurricular activities have lower-than-expected failure rates and higher-than-expected grades.[17] It could be that schools with greater club and team participation attract students who are generally more motivated, and this is why there is a relationship between club participation and school grades. However, another indicator of involvement that is not shown here—participation in out-of-school clubs—is not associated with higher grades. Instead, grades are higher in schools that are able to get more students involved in clubs and activities at the school. High involvement in tutoring, however, was not associated with higher grades, better attendance, or lower rates of failures than would be expected, given the students served by the school.

Finally, course performance was better than expected in schools with more cooperation among teachers—where teachers feel responsible for all students, and they trust and respect other teachers in the school—and where there is more coherence in programming in the school. These final relationships suggest that it is not just what happens in individual classrooms that matters, but how teachers work together in the school. *Coherence in instructional programming, in particular, is associated with higher grades and lower rates of failure.* This suggests caution if attempting to address problems of failure with programming that is disconnected from the core instructional work of the school. Schools in which teachers report less coherence among programs in the school have higher rates of course failure and lower grades. Attendance is also better where more teachers take collective responsibility for the academic success of students in the whole school—not just their own students.

In general, the factors that seem to matter the most for student success are those that are most in the control of the school. Only one climate measure associated with student characteristics is significantly associated with grades—the extent to which students support each other academically. None of the measures of parent support or parent interaction with teachers was significantly associated with grades or failures, once we control for student body composition. *Teachers working together in a coordinated way—taking responsibility for the whole school; providing relevant, coherent instruction; and developing strong relationships with students—most strongly distinguishes schools with above-expected student performance in their courses.*

All of these concepts are analyzed at the school level. Because students' experiences may vary widely within the same school, we expect that many of the school-related factors that affect student failure are difficult to discern if we only look at school averages. Students' absence rates and performance will depend on their cumulative experiences with specific teachers, peers, and school professionals. Still, these measures of the average climate in schools provide general evidence about what matters for course performance in the first year of high school. Other work being conducted at CCSR is examining the factors that affect students' grades in one class—eleventh-grade English. This work provides a more direct test of individual classroom climate on students' grades, and shows similar positive effects of classroom personalization on students' grades.[18]

### Chapter 3 Endnotes

1  Our reports of schools come from two sources, either students' reports about just one of their courses (English or math), or students' general reports about the school as a whole.
2  These are differences of two standard deviations across schools, taken from the square root of the level 2 variance shown in Table 7 in Appendix D.
3  Statistics on work are derived from the 2005 CCSR survey of CPS students. Even students who work more than ten hours per week miss just two more days of school per semester than students who do not work at all.
4  Analyses of surveys of eighth-graders show that students tend to attend higher-achieving high schools if they: attend an elementary school that tends to send students to high-achieving high schools, have more highly educated parents, report fewer disciplinary problems in elementary school, report some participation in religious organizations, and report more trust of their teachers in elementary school. These characteristics are also related to high school attendance rates.
5  In their description of schools with weak promoting power in New York, Balfanz and Legters (2004) show generally very low levels of entering achievement.
6  Models that allow the achievement coefficient to vary across schools show significant variation in the achievement-absence relationship across schools.
7  This is a difference of two standard deviations across schools, taken from the square root of the level 2 variance from Model 3. Absences were not controlled, since this is a behavior that occurs during high school, rather than a pre–high school characteristic. See Table 9 in Appendix D.
8  This is a difference of two standard deviations across schools, taken from the square root of the level 2 variance from Model 4.
9  In general, schools' average GPAs decrease as absence rates increase. However, if we compare students who have the same number of days absent, those who are at schools with poor attendance rates average higher GPAs than students with similar absences who are at schools with better average attendance. The relationship between absences and GPA decreases as school absence rates increase, so that more days of absence are associated with a smaller deficit at low-attendance schools compared to high-attendance schools. Students attending schools with high absence rates (one standard deviation above average) have GPAs that are 0.23 points higher, on average, than students with the same number of days absent who attend schools with low absence rates (one standard deviation below average).
10  We did not control for students' absences or study behaviors in the analysis of grades and failures because these are behaviors that occur after students have entered high school and are likely affected by their experiences in school. Therefore, many of the same factors that were associated with absences are also associated with grades and failures.
11  Pittman and Haughwout (1987); Wasley et al. (2000); Lee and Smith (1999); Lee and Burkam (2003); and Kahne, Sporte, and de la Torre (2006). In addition, two recent studies of dropout consisting of interviews with students (Boston Youth Transitions Task Force, 2006) and with dropouts (Bridgeland, Morison, and Dilulio; 2006) both concluded that relationships with teachers were one of the most important factors affecting students' school experiences.
12  This can be seen, for example, in qualitative work on freshman failure rates by Roderick (2005). She found that without knowing students personally, teachers were prone to attribute poor performance to lack of motivation, and so failed to help when students were experiencing particular stressors. Yet, students that high school teachers saw as unmotivated were sometimes rated as very motivated by their elementary teachers who knew them better. In contrast, students who formed a close relationship with an adult at the school were able to recover from failure in high school.
13  Marks et al. (1996); and Mitchell et al. (2005).
14  E.g., Letgers, Balfanz, and McPartland (2002); Shear et al. (2005); and Darling-Hammond, Ancess, and Wichterle Ort (2002).
15  Discussion of these issues is available in McDill, Natriello, and Pallas (1986) and McPartland and Schneider (1996).
16  Teachers' support of standards and testing is associated with lower grades, more failures, and higher absence rates. This might seem contradictory, but this measure is more of an indicator of teachers' feelings about testing and standards than a direct indicator of the demands placed on students. In fact, teachers may be more supportive of external guides in schools where they view demands to generally be weak.
17  We are not just saying that individual students who participate more in activities and tutoring have lower failure rates because we are measuring these relationships at the school level. Instead, attending a school where there is more overall participation in extracurricular activities and tutoring is associated with lower rates of course failure for all students.
18  Nagaoka and Deutsch (2006).

### Do Some Elementary Schools Do a Better Job Than Others at Preparing Their Students for the Transition to High School?

Elementary schools may prepare their students for high school in a number of ways. At the very least, elementary schools provide their students with the academic skills that they will need in high school. Students also develop other important skills in elementary school, such as attendance and studying habits, which they will need when they go to high school. At some elementary schools, staff members put effort into enrolling their students in high schools that they think will best serve them. Other elementary schools simply "feed" into specific high schools. Thus, the elementary school that students attend affects their enrollment at a specific high school. Finally, some elementary schools develop partnerships with the high schools to which they send many of their graduates; they may create transition programs for students or they may establish communication between elementary and high school teachers about the students they both serve. These different means of preparing students for high school are visible in students' freshman outcomes.

We can see differences across elementary schools in the degree to which their graduates perform well in their freshman-year courses. If we compare elementary schools by the average ninth-grade GPAs of their eighth-grade graduates, for example, they vary by about 0.67 points. This is about 10 percent of the total variation in students' GPAs.[A] Some of the differences among elementary schools can be attributed to which high schools students attend, either because of feeder patterns between elementary and high schools or because school staff members work to send their students to particular high schools. Once we account for students' high school enrollment, the differences across elementary schools in their graduates' ninth-grade performance shrink by half.[B] There are also differences in the background characteristics of students attending different elementary schools; after accounting for these differences in background characteristics (gender, race, and economic status), only about 2.3 percent of the total variation in freshman-year grades can be attributed to their elementary schools.

While 2.3 percent of the variation in grades is a small amount of the total variation, it is equivalent to a difference of about 0.32 GPA points. Some of these differences in students' high school grades result from different levels of academic preparation in elementary schools. Academic skills, as measured by students' test scores in eighth grade, explain an additional 0.4 percent of the variation in freshman GPAs across elementary schools (leaving 1.9 percent unexplained). Absence rates in the freshman year explain all but 0.07 percent of the remaining variation. There are only very small differences across elementary schools in their graduates' high school outcomes, once we account for high school enrollment, academic skills, and attendance patterns in high school. These remaining differences across elementary schools that are not explained by students' backgrounds, academic preparation, attendance, or high school enrollment are equivalent to about 0.16 GPA points. Thus, most of the effects of elementary schools on students' grades seem to work through traditional mechanisms: the high schools into which they send their graduates, the degree to which students leave with academic skills, and the degree to which their students have developed good habits with attendance and studying.

---

#### Sidebar Endnotes

A  This decomposition of variance comes from a two-level hierarchical linear model with students nested within elementary schools.

B  These statistics come from cross-nested hierarchical models with students nested simultaneously within elementary and high schools.

# Chapter 4

# Interpretive Summary

There is a growing consensus that we need to be concerned about students who fail to pass ninth grade because they are at high risk of not graduating.[1] Efforts to improve ninth-grade promotion rates tend to focus on students with few credits at the end of their first year in high school. But, as shown in Figure 7, even one failure in a full-year course (two semester courses) puts students at high risk of not graduating. In fact, students who receive only a few Fs, or who have very low grades with no Fs, may be the students most amenable to intervention because they are struggling but still making some progress in school. *We should pay attention to more than just the lowest-achieving students when working to address issues of graduation and dropping out.* In a school system where about half the students drop out, it is not just aberrant students who are at high risk of not graduating but average students as well.

## Problems of Failure and Dropping Out Are Embedded Within Issues of Improving Overall Achievement

Some educators may be concerned that efforts to improve dropout rates are contradictory to improving achievement. From this point of view, improving dropout rates means paying attention to the lowest-performing students—and these are the students who may be perceived as dragging down the achievement level of the school.[2] However, working to reduce dropouts does not just mean preventing failure among the lowest-achieving students. Students with few failures but poor grades in their classes are also at high risk of not graduating. Also, course failures are closely tied to overall performance—students who are failing any course also tend to do poorly in the classes they pass. Furthermore, the same school factors that are related to failures—student relationships with teachers and the degree to which school seems relevant to students—are also associated with higher grades.[3] Reducing dropout rates means improving course performance among all students—not just those with multiple course failures.

## Addressing Freshman Failures, Dropouts, and Achievement Requires a Critical Look at Core Practices That Affect Students' Grades in Their Courses

Current discussion about improving student achievement focuses on two broad areas: course rigor and accountability through high school testing. Efforts to address the dropout problem often entail special programs for failing students, flexible standards, or separate schools. None of these approaches requires a close examination of why students are performing poorly in their courses. For this reason, the effectiveness of these approaches may be limited.

It seems doubtful that increasing enrollment in rigorous courses, or emphasizing standardized testing, will greatly improve students' readiness for college or the workforce if students' course performance continues to be weak. For many years, CPS has had rigorous graduation requirements. Yet, of the students who graduate, over one-third leave school with no more than a D+ average.[4] Although these students participated in college preparatory coursework, they probably learned little with such poor performance. Likewise, standardized testing in the high schools has shown little academic benefit for students. The state of Illinois requires all CPS students to take the ACT examination at the end of eleventh grade. Despite substantial emphasis on preparation for this examination, 65 percent of CPS graduates receive a 17 or below, which is below all college-readiness benchmarks.[5] Research conducted by CCSR shows that these low scores are tied to poor performance in students' coursework. Students who receive higher marks in their courses show higher gains on corresponding standardized tests. *The strategies that are being proposed most strongly for high school reform must be accompanied with efforts to improve course performance (i.e., grades).* By themselves, rigorous requirements and standardized tests are unlikely to substantially raise student achievement.

Strategies for addressing dropout issues often entail special programs for at-risk students and multiple routes to graduation, splitting off students from the regular academic track.[6] The assumption behind such approaches is that off-track students are in need of a different type of education than regular students. This makes sense if there are a few students at risk of failure, but it is a questionable solution in typical schools where half the students eventually go off-track and fail to graduate. Addressing the educational needs of many

### We Are Not Suggesting That Students Be Given Passing Grades if They Have Not Shown Adequate Mastery of Course Material

The relationship between course Fs and graduation is strong, and knowledge of this relationship may tempt a sympathetic teacher to give a student credit even when standards for the class have not been met. We are not advocating this practice. To the contrary, such an action may demonstrate to the student that little effort is necessary for passing, thus making the student more likely to fail subsequent courses. We are also not suggesting that course requirements be "dumbed down" to make it easier for students to pass. If a class is too easy, students may lose motivation to attend; they may be more likely to fail not only that class but also subsequent classes that require the knowledge and skills they should have learned. Students may also be unprepared for subsequent demands in college or the labor market. Instead, we are advocating that teachers and schools identify students who are failing, find out why they are failing, and then try to give them the support they need to recover from this failure.

students at risk of not graduating requires systemic change to core practices in the school.[7]

Programmatic approaches to addressing dropping out are popular because they are easier to implement than systemic reforms,[8] and they target students who clearly need support. But besides being impractical in schools where most students go off-track, they are rarely found to be effective.[9] A "second chance" or "skimming off" strategy does little for students at risk for future failure, and it does not address problems of average and high-achieving students performing below their potential. Furthermore, too many options and programs may lead to confusion and poor choices among students who most need guidance and have the fewest supports.[10] Too many disconnected programs can also decrease coherence in the instructional program of the school.[11] This is not to say that programs and interventions for struggling students are not worthwhile; we certainly should be identifying students in need of support. But programs and interventions that are disconnected from the core instructional program of the school may not be the best use of resources. Flexibility and tailored programs for a few students should not substitute for critical evaluation of schools' instructional programming, and all programs should be developed to align coherently with the general instructional plan of the school.

At the beginning of this report, we noted that trying to address the myriad factors that affect students' decisions to leave school was an overwhelming task. If we add to this list separate efforts to address low achievement, the competing demands on schools can be enormous. But reducing dropout and increasing achievement both come down to the same thing: improving students' performance in their courses. *Figuring out how to help students do better in their courses and receive higher grades will simultaneously push students to higher levels of achievement (including student test scores) and keep more students in school.* Unfortunately, this is not a common theme in current discussions about high school reform.

Lack of attention to students' grades may exist because grades are viewed as subjective and unreliable. Standards may be somewhat lower in schools that primarily enroll low-achieving students; however, these differences seem to be modest. As shown in Figure 18, schools that enroll poorly prepared students do not have students graduating with high GPAs. Recall that grades strongly predict future outcomes, including college graduation and earnings in the workforce;[12] clearly they are valid as indicators of students' skills. Test scores are generally seen as objective measures across teachers, schools, and districts, but course grades are more predictive of future outcomes than test scores; they capture a broader range of skills measured over a longer period of time.

## Students Do Better in Their Coursework When They Have More Reasons to Come to Class and Work Hard

Students' academic preparation for high school is far less important for simply passing courses than is their behavior in high school, particularly their course attendance. *Course passing rates are primarily determined by attendance.* Almost all students who have good attendance finish their freshman year on-track. Schools know almost immediately which students are missing school or class, allowing them to determine why and develop strategies to improve attendance. This means working with students and parents, and it means thinking about attendance policies and instructional practices at the school.

*Students attend class more often when they have strong relationships with their teachers, and when they see school and their coursework as relevant and important for their future.* The relationships that students have with teachers and other adults at school provide encouragement to attend and support for academic learning and persistence. School itself could be seen as relevant and important for the future, providing students with motivation to attend. Individual coursework can also be perceived as relevant—helping students to grow and understand their world better or providing preparation for college and the workplace. The more students see their schoolwork as relevant for the future, the greater the likelihood that school as a whole will feel worthwhile. Other researchers who investigate high school reform have identified these same aspects of school climate—teacher-student relationships and the relevance of school for the future—as key in addressing issues of failure and dropout.[13] This study adds to that literature by providing quantitative evidence from a large sample of schools to support conclusions that have been drawn from case studies, focus groups, informal observations, and program evaluations. Taken together, there are consistent themes from many sources that freshman-year engagement and performance in school is higher in places with strong teacher-student relationships and where students see the relevance of what they are doing in school for their future.

But what does it mean to work on relationships and relevance in high schools? Does building relationships simply mean that teachers should be nice to students? Does increasing relevance mean introducing occasional units that are tied to work skills? Neither of those solutions seems adequate. Good relationships between teachers and students are not sufficient by themselves for high levels of student achievement or even for addressing high rates of failure. While successful programs often incorporate elements of personal relationships between teachers and students, programs that solely address relationships do not necessarily improve dropout rates or student achievement.[14] Likewise, it seems doubtful that student achievement or course performance would improve simply by introducing work-skill units or programs that are unconnected to the main academic content of students' classes. Instead, school-based relationships develop as teachers and students work together to meet academic goals. Relevance comes from making academic content meaningful to students.

A focus on students' course performance keeps attention on the factor that most directly affects graduation, and that simultaneously directly affects academic skills and postsecondary readiness. We can use course performance as a guide in two ways: identifying students who need support and identifying weaknesses in schools' instructional programming. In our previous report, we suggested that schools should be looking for patterns in student performance—by time of day, type of student, type of subject—to develop strategies to help schools identify particular groups of students, teachers, or structures that need attention. In this report, we have shown that there are a number of indicators of academic performance that can be used to identify students' risk of not graduating. Given what we know about what matters, schools may then ask: Is our instructional program set up to foster relationship building between school professionals and students? Are programs in the school organized coherently around students' academic performance? Are students being monitored and provided supports as needed? Are teachers receiving feedback and support for relationship building with students and instructional relevance?

Grades and attendance in CPS are alarmingly low, even among students testing above national norms in the eighth grade. Boys are doing particularly poorly, and not because they are studying or attending school much less than girls. In addition, nonwhite students, who make up the majority of the CPS student population, receive lower grades than white students after adjustments are made for elementary test scores, economic background, attendance, and study behavior. Poor course performance is a critical issue for CPS, and we need a better understanding of why some subgroups of students show particularly low grades. Traditional explanations—such as low motivation, attendance, or work effort—do not explain the discrepancies.

## Efforts to Improve High School Course Performance Do Not Rest Solely With High Schools

Very good grades in high school are unlikely unless students have shown strong academic performance in elementary school; this suggests that high schools cannot address this issue alone. *Elementary and middle schools should work with high schools to prepare students for the ninth-grade transition.* Academic preparation in elementary school is also related to attendance in high school—students entering high school with high achievement are less likely to have serious absence problems in high school than moderate or low-achieving students. Neild and Balfanz (2006) have shown that attendance and failure in eighth grade can be used to predict eventual dropout. Currently, CPS puts students in high school preparatory programs by their test scores, but why not use criteria, such as attendance and grades, that are more predictive of success? Elementary teachers tend to know their students better than high school teachers. CPS might consider building communication between middle school and high school teachers regarding expectations and supports for students in the transition to high school.[15]

*We also need to actively spread the message to students and parents that grades and attendance matter a great deal.* Attendance is the most important determinant of passing classes and graduating. Even a week of absence per semester substantially increases the likelihood of failing a class. More importantly, grades are the most important determinant of graduating from high school, going to college, and graduating from college. Students who want to graduate from college—78 percent of CPS seniors—should be aiming for B or higher averages in high school. The vast majority of CPS students want to go to college, and their parents support this goal. They should know that achieving this goal requires strong performance in high school coursework. All students should be working for regular attendance and high grades.

### Chapter 4 Endnotes

1  See discussion of the ninth-grade graduation link in reports by the National Association of Secondary School Principals (2005), the *American School Board Journal* (Black, 2004) and Achieve, Inc. (Jerald, 2006), and research by Neild and Balfanz (2006), and Cahill, Hamilton, and Lynch (2006).
2  See Roderick, Nagaoka, and Allensworth (2006) for a more detailed discussion of perceptions of the trade-off between high standards and diploma attainment.
3  To be certain that the analyses of grades were not being overly influenced by the factors that affect course failure, identical analyses were performed predicting grades in the courses that students passed. The results were almost identical to those that incorporated failures.
4  Roderick, Nagaoka, and Allensworth (2006).
5  Ibid. Scores below 17 place students in the bottom quartile of students taking the ACT examination. According to ACT guidelines, students should score an 18 on the English portion of the test to have a 50 percent chance of obtaining a B or higher in college English and a 22 on the math portion to have a 50 percent chance of obtaining a B or higher in college algebra.
6  For example, one of the main recommendations in a recent report of the National Association of Secondary School Principals (2005) was that routes toward graduation be flexible; for example, that there be loose standards for grade promotion. These suggestions echo plans here in Chicago. Likewise, several programs place struggling students into special classes and schools; for example, this is the strategy that New York is taking for students at risk of dropping out. See Cahill, Hamilton, and Lynch (2006).
7  The suggestion that we pay attention to core practices of the school, rather than just seeing dropout behavior as embedded within students, echoes a recommendation made by Lee and Burkam (2003) after their research showed that dropping out was related to high school organization and structure.
8  In his essay on how to address dropout, Rumbuger (2006) describes evidence for programmatic and systemic approaches for addressing dropouts. He notes that there is little evidence that programmatic solutions are generally effective, but that systematic approaches may often be too difficult to implement.
9  Dynarski (2004).
10  In Chicago, for example, graduation rates improved when all students were required to take a college-preparatory sequence and enroll in seven credits their freshman year. Prior to the new requirements, many students took too few courses to graduate on time.
11  Grades and failure rates are better in schools with strong coherence in instructional programming. In addition to evidence presented in this report, the importance of coherence in instructional programming is echoed in work we have done in elementary schools. See Newmann, Smith, Allensworth, and Bryk (2002).
12  Roderick, Nagaoka, and Allensworth (2006); Noble and Sawyer (2002); and Miller (1998).
13  A number of high school reform models that incorporate elements of personal relationships between teachers and students, as well as connections between school and the future, have been shown to be successful for addressing issues of dropout and freshman failure. For example, evaluations of AVID and Talent Development—programs that emphasize strong social support among students and teachers—have shown improvements in attendance, achievement, and dropout rates. See Watt, Powell, and Mendiola (2004); and McParland, Balfanz, Jordan, and Legters (1998). From evaluations of four high school reform models (including Talent Development), researchers at MDRC concluded that improvements in graduation rates can occur with instructional improvement that includes increased personalization and supports for struggling students See Herlihy and Quint (2006). In their review of six effective dropout prevention and college attendance programs for at-risk students, Fashola and Slavin (1998) found that the successful programs had several elements in common, including personalization between students and teachers, connections to an attainable future, and academic assistance to help students succeed in rigorous (not remedial) classes. In a large quantitative study of schools in Maryland, Kerr and Letgers (2004) found that those with small learning communities have lower dropout rates than expected, and attribute this to improved personalization. Based on their observations of schools that "beat the odds" in terms of freshman promotion rates, Balfanz and Letgers (2006) suggested that instruction should be connected to higher education and the workplace, as well as tied to support. Case studies of the freshman transition by Roderick (2005), as well as interviews with dropouts (Bridgeland, Morison, and Dilulio, 2006), and interviews with students, parents, and teachers (Boston Youth Transitions Task Force, 2006), all emphasize the importance of teacher-student relationships for addressing issues of failure and/or dropout. Using a large quantitative national database, Lee and Burkam (2003) likewise found teacher-student relationships to significantly affect dropout rates.
14  See Dynarski's (2004) review of dropout prevention programs. In Chicago, the initiative to break down large schools into smaller schools succeeded in improving personalization and relationships between teachers and students, but student achievement remained very low. See Kahne, Sporte, and de la Torre (2006). The small school initiative in Chicago has recognized the need to focus on instructional improvement in the schools.
15  There is evidence that middle school transition programs can help students in their freshman year. See Mizelle and Irvin (2000); and Hertzog and Morgan (1999).

## A Summary Model of High School Effects on Student Outcomes

Preparing high school students for college and labor market success is the key concern of high school reform, and graduating from high school is the minimum requirement that students need to achieve post-secondary success. We began this report by suggesting that we could address low graduation rates by focusing on students' performance in their classes. Here, we summarize our findings with the aid of a diagram (Figure 22). Our key outcome is high school graduation, which is shown on the far right of the chart. It is embedded within college and labor market readiness as the most basic indicator of preparation that students obtain from high school.

To get to graduation, students need to accumulate sufficient credits over at least four years. Passing classes is essential for accumulating credits, and students' performance in their freshman year affects their likelihood of success in the subsequent years of high school. Figure 22 shows this sequence; passing classes and credit accumulation are shown as *embedded within* general academic performance. Reducing failure and increasing credit accumulation are both about improving achievement.

Often we think of graduation as an outcome that results from many different influences—family, peers, community, schools—and it can seem like an overwhelming problem to try to manage. Yet, while all of these background factors are related to a student's likelihood of graduating, their influence works primarily through class performance; thus, the arrows in the diagram that show the influence of pre–high school characteristics do not point directly to graduation but to the boxes that precede graduation. This suggests two potential mechanisms for improving graduation rates. At the very least, by looking at students' course performance as early as freshman year we can identify students at risk of not graduating who need the most support. We can tell which students are likely not to graduate from observable data that are readily available to schools. At the most, the effect that schools and teachers can have on course performance, beyond the influence of background factors and preparation, provides a direct lever to work on graduation rates—a lever that is more accessible to school professionals than personal or family factors, and that is more strongly tied to graduation than nonacademic factors.

**FIGURE 22**

**A Summary of High School Effects on Student Outcomes**

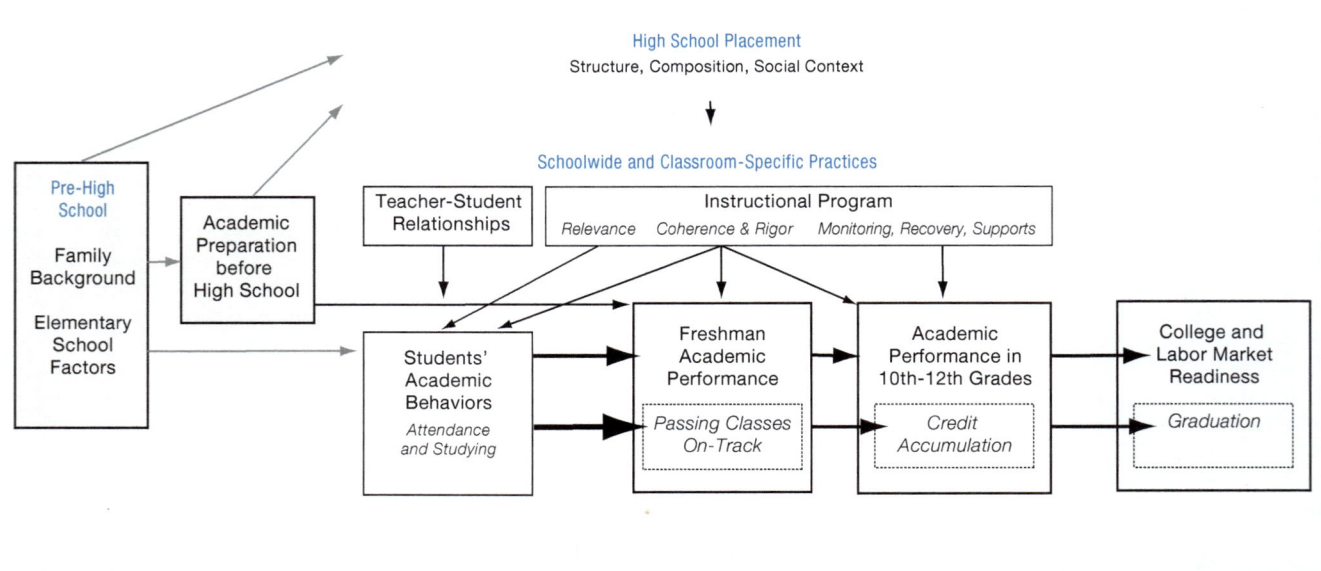

Students' academic preparation for high school and their background characteristics affect students' likelihood of graduating in several ways. First, they affect the development of academic skills and behaviors that students will need in high school. The development of appropriate behaviors is particularly important because passing courses depends primarily on students' behaviors in high school. Failure is overwhelmingly tied to attendance, and this is represented by a thick arrow from attendance to passing classes and on-track in Figure 22. Higher achievement is also strongly determined by students' behaviors in high school, but high grades are unlikely if students do not also have good academic preparation prior to high school.

Students' backgrounds and academic performance in elementary school also affect high school outcomes by leading students to enroll in specific high schools. Some schools are only accessible to high-achieving students, while enrollment in other schools depends on students' residential location or on student and parental efforts to enroll in non-neighborhood schools. High school climate and practices, in turn, affect students' performance in their coursework. Many aspects of high school climate are affected by the composition of students who enroll in the school. However, even among schools serving similar student populations, there are differences in practices that affect students' performance in their coursework.

Inside the school, relationships with teachers and peers provide students with reasons for coming to class and putting forth effort, while relationships in the larger school can provide motivation for attending school. Students are more likely to put forth effort if they view the work they are doing in their classes as relevant for their future, and if they are being pushed by the school to have high aspirations and make plans for the future. When schools can make the connection of high school work to students' futures, students are most likely to put forth effort to succeed.

Relevance is just one feature of the instructional program of a school, which includes the rigor and coherence of classroom instruction, and the rigor and coherence of the broader instructional plan of the school. Rigor and coherence affect the extent to which students' effort and preparation translate into learning through challenging, coherent content and tasks.

An additional component of instructional programming that we did not measure in our surveys is the extent to which schools monitor student progress and provide supports that allow students to recover from failure. We include these elements in Figure 22 because work by other scholars has suggested that schools can help students improve their academic performance through careful monitoring and support.[A] At the classroom level, monitoring student achievement and developing methods for recovery, which is part of individualization and personalization of instruction, is facilitated by close relationships between teachers and students. Monitoring can also occur at the school level, with principals and counselors using data on course performance to identify students performing below expectations and developing plans for summer school, tutoring, and course scheduling.

Improving students' course performance is a key mechanism for improving both graduation rates and academic achievement. This requires critical examination of core practices across the school and in individual classrooms—the extent to which instruction is relevant, coherent, and rigorous—along with attempts to ensure monitoring and support for struggling students, as well as to build good relationships between teachers and students.

---

### Sidebar Endnotes

[A] In their observations of schools that "beat the odds" in terms of ninth-grade promotion, Balfanz and Letgers (2006) found not only that they had strong instructional programs and a personalized structure but also that they had monitoring systems to get students back on-track.

# References

ACT (2005)
*ACT college readiness benchmarks, retention, and first-year college GPA: What's the connection?* Available online at http://www.act.org/path/policy/pdf/2005-2.pdf.

Akey, Theresa M. (2006)
*School context, student attitudes and behavior, and academic achievement: An exploratory analysis.* New York: MDRC. Available online at www.mdrc.org/publications/419/full.pdf.

Alexander, Karl L., Doris R. Entwisle, and S. L. Dauber (2003)
*On the success of failure: A reassessment of the effects of retention in the primary grades.* Cambridge, Mass.: Cambridge University Press.

Alexander, Karl L., Doris R. Entwisle, and Nader S. Kabbani (2001)
*Teachers College Record.* New York: Teachers College. 103: 760–822.

Allensworth, Elaine M. (2004)
*Ending social promotion: The effects of retention.* Chicago: Consortium on Chicago School Research at the University of Chicago.

Allensworth, Elaine M. (2005)
*Graduation and dropout trends in Chicago: A look at cohorts of students from 1991 through 2004.* Chicago: Consortium on Chicago School Research at the University of Chicago.

Allensworth, Elaine M., and John Q. Easton (2005)
*The On-Track Indicator as a Predictor of High School Graduation.* Chicago: Consortium on Chicago School Research.

Balfanz, Robert, and Nettie E. Legters (2004)
*Locating the dropout crisis: Which high schools produced the nation's dropouts? Where are they located? Who attends them?* Baltimore, Md.: Johns Hopkins University.

Balfanz, Robert, and Nettie E. Legters (2006)
*Closing 'dropout factories': the graduation-rate crisis we know, and what can be done about it.* Baltimore, Md.: Johns Hopkins University. July.

Balfanz, Robert, Nettie E. Legters, and James M. McPartland (2002)
*Solutions for failing high schools: Converging visions and promising models.* Center for Social Organization of Schools/Johns Hopkins University. March.

Balfanz, Robert, and Ruth C. Neild (2006)
An extreme degree of difficulty: The educational demographics of urban neighborhood high schools. *Journal of Education for Students Placed at Risk,* 11(2): 123–41.

Balfanz, Robert, and Ruth C. Neild (2006)
*Unfulfilled promise: The dimensions and characteristics of Philadelphia's dropout crisis, 2000–2005.*

Barton, Paul E. (2005)
*One-third of a nation: Rising dropout rates and declining opportunities.* February. Princeton, N.J.: Educational Testing Services.

Black, Susan (2004)
The pivotal year. *American School Board Journal,* 191(02). From www.asbj.com/2004/02/0204research.html (accessed October 11, 2004).

Boston Youth Transitions Task Force (2006)
*Too big to be seen: The invisible dropout crisis in Boston and America.* May.

Bridgeland, John M., Karen B. Morison, and John J. Dilulio (2006)
*The silent epidemic: Perspectives of high school dropouts.* Washington, D.C.: A report by Civic Enterprises in Association with Peter D. Hart Research Associates for the Bill and Melinda Gates Foundation. March.

Brooks, David (2006)
The gender gap. *New York Times,* June 11.

Cahill, Michele, Leah Hamilton, and JoEllen Lynch (2006)
*Summary findings and strategic solutions for overage, under-credited youth.* New York City Department of Education.

Darling-Hammond, Linda, Jacqueline Ancess, and Susanna Wichterle Ort (2002)
Reinventing high school: Outcomes of the Coalition Campus Schools Project. *American Educational Research Journal,* 39(3): 639–73.

Dee, Thomas S. (2005)
*Teachers and the gender gaps in student achievement.* NBER Working Paper No. W11660, September. Available online at http://ssrn.com/abstract=819821.

Duckworth, Angela Lee, and Martin E. P. Seligman (2006)
Self-discipline gives girls the edge: Gender in self-discipline, grades, and achievement test scores. *Journal of Educational Psychology,* 98(1): 198–208.

Dynarski, Mark (2004)
"Interpreting the evidence from recent federal evaluations of dropout-prevention programs: The state of scientific research" in Gary Orfield (Ed.) *Dropouts in America: Confronting the graduation rate crisis,* pp. 255–67. Cambridge, Mass.: Harvard Education Press.

Fashola, Olatokunbo S., and Robert E. Slavin (1998)
Effective dropout prevention and college attendance programs for students placed at risk. *Journal of Education for Students Placed at Risk,* 3(2): 159–83.

Greene, Jay P., and Marcus A. Winters (2006)
*Leaving boys behind: Public high school graduation rates,* Manhattan Institute Civic Report 48, April.

Grissom, James B., and Lorrie A. Shepard (1989)
Repeating and dropping out of school. In L. A. Shepard and M. L. Smith (Ed.) *Flunking grades: Research and policies on retention.* London: Falmer Press.

Herlihy, Corinne M., and Janet Quint (2006)
*Emerging evidence on improving high school student achievement and graduation rates: The effects of four popular improvement programs.* National High School Center.

Hertzog, C. Jay, and P. Lena Morgan (1999)
Making the transition from middle level to high school, *High School Magazine,* 6(4): 26–30.

Jerald, Craig D. (2006)
*Identifying potential dropouts: Key lessons for building an early warning data system.* June. Achieve, Inc.

Kahne, Joseph E., Sue Sporte, and Marisa de la Torre (2006)
*Small schools on a larger scale: The first three years of the Chicago High School Redesign Initiative.* Chicago: Consortium on Chicago School Research at the University of Chicago.

Kerr, Kerri A., and Nettie E. Letgers (2004)
Preventing dropout: Use and impact of organizational reforms designed to ease the transition to high school. In Gary Orfield (Ed.) *Dropouts in America: Confronting the graduation rate crisis,* pp. 221–42. Cambridge, Mass.: Harvard Education Press.

Lee, Valerie E., and David T. Burkam (2003)
Dropping out of high school: The role of school organization and structure. *American Education Research Journal,* 40(2): 353–93.

Lee, Valerie E., and Julia B. Smith (1999)
Social support and achievement for young adolescents in Chicago: The role of school academic press. *American Educational Research Journal,* 36(4): 907–45.

Letgers, Nettie E., Robert Balfanz, and James M. McPartland (2002)
*Solutions for failing high schools: Converging visions and promising models.* Available online at http://www.ed.gov/offices/OVAE/HS/legters.doc.

Leving, Jeffery M., and Glenn Sacks (2006)
Resolving the boy crisis in schools. *Chicago Sun-Times.* May 7.

McPartland, James M., Robert Balfanz, Will J. Jordan, and Nettie E. Letgers (1998)
Improving climate and achievement in a troubled urban high school through the Talent Development Model. *Journal of Education for Students Placed at Risk,* 3(4): 337–311.

McPartland, James M. and Will J. Jordan (2004)
Essential components of high school dropout-prevention reforms. In Gary Orfield (Ed.) *Dropouts in America: Confronting the graduation rate crisis,* pp. 269–88. Cambridge, Mass.: Harvard Education Press.

Miller, Shazia R. (1998)
High school grades as a signal of human capital. EEPA, 20(4): 299–311.

Mizelle, Nancy B., and Judith L. Irvin (2000)
Transition from middle school into high school. *Middle School Journal,* 31(5): 1–8.

Nagaoka, Jenny, and Jonah Deutsch (2007)
*The ABCs of grades: How order, expectations, and demands affect them.* Paper presented at the meetings of the American Educational Research Association, Chicago.

National Association of Secondary School Principals (2005)
*What counts: Defining and improving high school graduation rates.* Reston, Va.

National Center for Education Statistics, U.S. Department of Education (2007)
*Course credit accrual and dropping out of high school.* Washington, D.C.: NCES 2007–018.

Newacheck, Paul W., et al. (1998)
An epidemiologic profile of children with special health care needs. *Pediatrics,* 102(1): 1998, 117–23.

Newmann, Fred M., et al. (2002)
Improving Chicago's Schools: School Instructional Program Coherence. *ERS Spectrum: Journal of School Research and Information,* 20(2): 38–46.

Noble, Julie, and Richard Sawyer (2002)
*Predicting different levels of academic success in college using high school GPA and ACT composite score.* Available online at http://www.act.org/research/reports/pdf/ACT_RR2002-4.pdf.

Orfield, Gary (2004)
Losing our future: Minority youth left out. In Gary Orfield (Ed.) *Dropouts in America: Confronting the graduation rate crisis,* pp. 1–11. Cambridge, Mass.: Harvard Education Press.

Patterson, Orlando (2006)
A poverty of the mind. *New York Times.* March 20.

Promising Practices Network on Children, Families, and Communities (2005)
*Proven and Promising Programs: Benchmark.*

Roderick, Melissa (1994)
Grade retention and school dropout: Investigating the association. *American Educational Research Journal,* 31(4): 729–59.

Roderick, Melissa (2005)
What's happening to the boys? Early high school experiences and school outcomes among African-American male adolescents in Chicago. In Olatokunbo S. Fashola, (Ed.) *Educating African-American males: Voices from the field,* pp. 151–227. Thousand Oaks, Calif.: Sage Publications.

Roderick, Melissa, and Eric Camburn (1999)
Risk and recovery from course failure in the early years of high school. *American Educational Research Journal,* 36(2): 303–43.

Roderick, Melissa, and Jenny Nagaoka (2004)
*Ending social promotion: The effects of retention.* Chicago: Consortium on Chicago School Research at the University of Chicago.

Roderick, Melissa, Jenny Nagaoka, and Elaine M. Allensworth (2006)
*From high schools to the future: A first look at Chicago public school graduates' college enrollment, college preparation, and graduation from four-year colleges.* Chicago: Consortium on Chicago School Research at the University of Chicago.

Rumberger, Russell (2004a)
Why students drop out of school. In Gary Orfield (Ed.) *Dropouts in America: Confronting the graduation rate crisis,* pp. 131–55. Cambridge, Mass.: Harvard Education Press.

Rumberger, Russell (2004b)
What can be done to reduce the dropout rate? In Gary Orfield (Ed.) *Dropouts in America: Confronting the graduation rate crisis,* pp. 243–54. Cambridge, Mass.: Harvard Education Press.

Shear, Linda, et al. (2005)
*Creating cultures for learning: Supportive relationships in new and redesigned high schools.* Washington, D.C., and Menlo Park, Calif.: American Institutes for Research and SRI International. Available online at www.gatesfoundation.org/nr/downloads/ed/evaluation/Year%203%20Final%20Reports/Relationship%20Rpt%2010_21.pdf.

Starfield, Barbara (1982)
Family income, ill health, and medical care of U.S. children. *Journal of Public Health Policy.*

Swanson, Christopher B. (2004)
Sketching a portrait of public high school graduation: Who graduates? Who doesn't? In Gary Orfield (Ed.) *Dropouts in America: Confronting the graduation rate crisis,* pp. 13–40. Cambridge, Mass.: Harvard Education Press.

Tyre, Peg (2006)
The trouble with boys. *Newsweek,* pp. 44–52, January 30.

Watt, Karen M., Charles A. Powell, and Irma Doris Mendiola (2004)
Implications of one comprehensive school reform model for secondary school students underrepresented in higher education. *Journal of Education for Students Placed at Risk (JESPAR),* 9(3): 241–59.

# Appendix A: Individual School Data

**TABLE 2**
**Data for Figure 17 and Figure 18**

| School Name | Average Incoming Math Achievement in the School | Eighth-Grade Math Test Scores, National Quartile | Average Number of Days Absent | Average GPA |
|---|---|---|---|---|
| Amundsen | 251 | Bottom | 12.6 | 1.6 |
| Amundsen | 251 | Second | 10.0 | 1.9 |
| Amundsen | 251 | Third | 7.8 | 2.3 |
| Amundsen | 251 | Top | 6.5 | 2.6 |
| Bogan | 246 | Bottom | 15.8 | 1.1 |
| Bogan | 246 | Second | 12.8 | 1.4 |
| Bogan | 246 | Third | 9.3 | 1.9 |
| Bogan | 246 | Top | 9.8 | 2.0 |
| Brooks | 282 | Top | 2.7 | 2.5 |
| Carver | 239 | Bottom | 10.5 | 1.3 |
| Carver | 239 | Second | 9.1 | 1.7 |
| Chicago Agricultural | 265 | Third | 4.1 | 2.1 |
| Clark | 249 | Second | 7.2 | 1.8 |
| Clark | 249 | Third | 5.6 | 2.1 |
| Clemente | 243 | Bottom | 11.3 | 1.7 |
| Clemente | 243 | Second | 8.7 | 1.7 |
| Clemente | 243 | Third | 7.4 | 2.1 |
| Clemente | 243 | Top | 7.3 | 2.2 |
| Collins | 228 | Bottom | 17.7 | 1.3 |
| Collins | 228 | Second | 15.5 | 1.6 |
| Corliss | 236 | Bottom | 16.0 | 1.3 |
| Corliss | 236 | Second | 10.5 | 1.8 |
| Corliss | 236 | Third | 9.0 | 2.1 |
| Crane | 232 | Bottom | 17.4 | 1.4 |
| Crane | 232 | Second | 11.7 | 1.8 |
| Crane | 232 | Third | 10.5 | 2.2 |
| Crane Achievement Academy | 220 | Bottom | 20.3 | 1.3 |

*Continued on next page*

**TABLE 2—CONTINUED**

**Data for Figure 17 and Figure 18**

| School Name | Average Incoming Math Achievement in the School | Eighth-Grade Math Test Scores, National Quartile | Average Number of Days Absent | Average GPA |
|---|---|---|---|---|
| Curie | 262 | Bottom | 4.5 | 2.1 |
| Curie | 262 | Second | 5.4 | 2.0 |
| Curie | 262 | Third | 4.5 | 2.4 |
| Curie | 262 | Top | 3.5 | 2.7 |
| CVS | 246 | Bottom | 16.7 | 1.3 |
| CVS | 246 | Second | 15.3 | 1.4 |
| CVS | 246 | Third | 13.2 | 1.6 |
| CVS | 246 | Top | 12.5 | 1.8 |
| CVS Achievement Academy | 220 | Bottom | 19.4 | 1.2 |
| CVS Achievement Academy | 220 | Second | 16.7 | 1.5 |
| Douglass Middle | 226 | Bottom | 15.7 | 1.4 |
| Dunbar | 245 | Bottom | 13.3 | 1.5 |
| Dunbar | 245 | Second | 11.7 | 1.7 |
| Dunbar | 245 | Third | 9.4 | 2.1 |
| Englewood | 228 | Bottom | 17.2 | 1.4 |
| Englewood | 228 | Second | 15.3 | 1.7 |
| Englewood | 228 | Third | 10.8 | 2.2 |
| Farragut | 239 | Bottom | 13.3 | 1.2 |
| Farragut | 239 | Second | 9.5 | 1.8 |
| Farragut | 239 | Third | 7.0 | 2.3 |
| Farragut | 239 | Top | 5.5 | 2.6 |
| Fenger | 231 | Bottom | 14.3 | 1.7 |
| Fenger | 231 | Second | 13.0 | 1.8 |
| Fenger | 231 | Third | 13.5 | 2.0 |
| Foreman | 238 | Bottom | 12.8 | 1.5 |
| Foreman | 238 | Second | 10.4 | 1.5 |
| Foreman | 238 | Third | 7.7 | 1.9 |
| Gage Park | 242 | Bottom | 12.4 | 1.6 |
| Gage Park | 242 | Second | 12.6 | 1.7 |
| Gage Park | 242 | Third | 8.1 | 2.1 |
| Hancock | 248 | Second | 10.1 | 1.6 |
| Harlan | 237 | Bottom | 14.3 | 1.5 |
| Harlan | 237 | Second | 9.8 | 2.0 |
| Harlan | 237 | Third | 10.0 | 2.2 |
| Harper | 227 | Bottom | 10.6 | 1.3 |
| Harper | 227 | Second | 8.9 | 1.7 |
| Harper | 227 | Third | 7.7 | 1.8 |
| Hirsch | 234 | Bottom | 12.7 | 1.2 |
| Hirsch | 234 | Second | 11.4 | 1.5 |

*Continued on next page*

## TABLE 2–CONTINUED
### Data for Figure 17 and Figure 18

| School Name | Average Incoming Math Achievement in the School | Eighth-Grade Math Test Scores, National Quartile | Average Number of Days Absent | Average GPA |
|---|---|---|---|---|
| **Hope** | 263 | Third | 4.6 | 2.3 |
| Hope | 263 | Top | 3.2 | 2.7 |
| **Hubbard** | 255 | Bottom | 14.5 | 1.3 |
| Hubbard | 255 | Second | 9.6 | 1.8 |
| Hubbard | 255 | Third | 6.8 | 2.2 |
| Hubbard | 255 | Top | 5.8 | 2.6 |
| **Hyde Park** | 246 | Bottom | 18.0 | 1.1 |
| Hyde Park | 246 | Second | 13.3 | 1.6 |
| Hyde Park | 246 | Third | 9.9 | 2.2 |
| Hyde Park | 246 | Top | 7.3 | 2.6 |
| **Jones** | 294 | Top | 2.3 | 2.8 |
| **Juarez** | 244 | Bottom | 8.4 | 1.4 |
| Juarez | 244 | Second | 8.0 | 1.7 |
| Juarez | 244 | Third | 6.3 | 2.0 |
| **Julian** | 247 | Bottom | 11.8 | 1.3 |
| Julian | 247 | Second | 9.8 | 1.5 |
| Julian | 247 | Third | 8.8 | 1.7 |
| **Kelly** | 249 | Bottom | 12.5 | 1.3 |
| Kelly | 249 | Second | 9.2 | 1.7 |
| Kelly | 249 | Third | 7.0 | 2.1 |
| Kelly | 249 | Top | 5.0 | 2.5 |
| **Kelvyn Park** | 242 | Bottom | 12.2 | 1.6 |
| Kelvyn Park | 242 | Second | 11.1 | 1.9 |
| Kelvyn Park | 242 | Third | 10.6 | 2.2 |
| **Kennedy** | 253 | Bottom | 10.1 | 1.6 |
| Kennedy | 253 | Second | 9.3 | 1.7 |
| Kennedy | 253 | Third | 7.2 | 2.2 |
| Kennedy | 253 | Top | 5.3 | 2.7 |
| **Kenwood** | 258 | Bottom | 16.9 | 1.0 |
| Kenwood | 258 | Second | 9.5 | 1.8 |
| Kenwood | 258 | Third | 6.8 | 2.1 |
| Kenwood | 258 | Top | 5.4 | 2.4 |
| **Martin Luther King** | 274 | Third | 3.0 | 2.5 |
| Martin Luther King | 274 | Top | 3.6 | 2.5 |
| **Lake View** | 258 | Second | 7.1 | 2.1 |
| Lake View | 258 | Third | 6.4 | 2.5 |
| Lake View | 258 | Top | 5.1 | 2.9 |
| **Lane Tech** | 289 | Third | 3.1 | 2.6 |
| Lane Tech | 289 | Top | 2.5 | 2.7 |

*Continued on next page*

**TABLE 2—CONTINUED**

## Data for Figure 17 and Figure 18

| School Name | Average Incoming Math Achievement in the School | Eighth-Grade Math Test Scores, National Quartile | Average Number of Days Absent | Average GPA |
|---|---|---|---|---|
| Lincoln Park | 271 | Second | 9.7 | 1.9 |
| Lincoln Park | 271 | Third | 7.0 | 2.2 |
| Lincoln Park | 271 | Top | 3.1 | 2.8 |
| Manley | 233 | Bottom | 9.1 | 1.5 |
| Manley | 233 | Second | 9.8 | 1.7 |
| Manley | 233 | Third | 8.2 | 2.0 |
| Marshall | 231 | Bottom | 16.1 | 1.2 |
| Marshall | 231 | Second | 12.2 | 1.6 |
| Marshall | 231 | Third | 10.6 | 1.9 |
| Mather | 250 | Bottom | 11.1 | 1.5 |
| Mather | 250 | Second | 8.5 | 1.8 |
| Mather | 250 | Third | 6.6 | 2.2 |
| Mather | 250 | Top | 7.7 | 2.3 |
| Morgan Park | 263 | Bottom | 13.2 | 1.1 |
| Morgan Park | 263 | Second | 9.6 | 1.6 |
| Morgan Park | 263 | Third | 5.6 | 2.1 |
| Morgan Park | 263 | Top | 4.6 | 2.5 |
| Moses Vines | 230 | Bottom | 11.8 | 1.7 |
| North-Grand | 241 | Bottom | 3.4 | 2.2 |
| North-Grand | 241 | Second | 2.9 | 2.7 |
| North-Grand | 241 | Third | 2.2 | 3.2 |
| Northside Prep | 308 | Top | 0.6 | 3.3 |
| Payton | 298 | Top | 1.9 | 3.1 |
| Phillips | 227 | Bottom | 16.7 | 1.5 |
| Phillips | 227 | Second | 15.2 | 1.6 |
| Prosser | 266 | Third | 5.6 | 2.3 |
| Prosser | 266 | Top | 5.3 | 2.5 |
| Robeson | 224 | Bottom | 19.4 | 1.2 |
| Robeson | 224 | Second | 14.9 | 1.7 |
| Robeson Achievement Academy | 216 | Bottom | 16.7 | 1.6 |
| Roosevelt | 241 | Bottom | 12.3 | 1.5 |
| Roosevelt | 241 | Second | 10.7 | 1.7 |
| Roosevelt | 241 | Third | 8.4 | 2.0 |
| School of Arts | 225 | Bottom | 13.4 | 1.5 |
| Schurz | 246 | Bottom | 11.7 | 1.3 |
| Schurz | 246 | Second | 11.2 | 1.5 |
| Schurz | 246 | Third | 8.3 | 2.0 |
| Schurz | 246 | Top | 8.0 | 2.2 |

*Continued on next page*

**TABLE 2–CONTINUED**

### Data for Figure 17 and Figure 18

| School Name | Average Incoming Math Achievement in the School | Eighth-Grade Math Test Scores, National Quartile | Average Number of Days Absent | Average GPA |
|---|---|---|---|---|
| Senn | 240 | Bottom | 13.1 | 1.3 |
| Senn | 240 | Second | 8.6 | 1.8 |
| Senn | 240 | Third | 8.2 | 2.0 |
| Simeon | 258 | Second | 5.6 | 1.9 |
| Simeon | 258 | Third | 4.6 | 2.1 |
| Simeon | 258 | Top | 5.4 | 2.1 |
| Steinmetz | 250 | Bottom | 13.9 | 1.3 |
| Steinmetz | 250 | Second | 11.7 | 1.4 |
| Steinmetz | 250 | Third | 8.2 | 1.9 |
| Steinmetz | 250 | Top | 6.4 | 2.2 |
| Sullivan | 244 | Bottom | 11.3 | 1.3 |
| Sullivan | 244 | Second | 9.9 | 1.5 |
| Sullivan | 244 | Third | 6.6 | 2.1 |
| Taft | 257 | Bottom | 11.1 | 1.4 |
| Taft | 257 | Second | 9.3 | 1.5 |
| Taft | 257 | Third | 8.3 | 1.9 |
| Taft | 257 | Top | 6.4 | 2.3 |
| Technology | 227 | Bottom | 13.3 | 1.3 |
| Tilden | 226 | Bottom | 20.0 | 1.2 |
| Tilden | 226 | Second | 18.0 | 1.5 |
| Tilden | 226 | Third | 17.5 | 1.8 |
| Tilden Achievement Academy | 221 | Bottom | 18.6 | 1.2 |
| Von Steuben | 269 | Second | 6.3 | 1.7 |
| Von Steuben | 269 | Third | 5.3 | 2.1 |
| Von Steuben | 269 | Top | 4.6 | 2.4 |
| Washington | 252 | Bottom | 10.5 | 1.5 |
| Washington | 252 | Second | 12.0 | 1.5 |
| Washington | 252 | Third | 7.8 | 2.0 |
| Washington | 252 | Top | 6.7 | 2.3 |
| Wells | 239 | Bottom | 12.3 | 1.5 |
| Wells | 239 | Second | 10.1 | 1.9 |
| Wells | 239 | Third | 9.2 | 2.1 |
| Westinghouse Achievement Academy | 217 | Bottom | 18.1 | 1.4 |
| Young | 301 | Top | 2.3 | 3.0 |

# Appendix B: Description of Survey Measures

**TABLE 3**

**CCSR Measures on School Climate and Instruction**

| Measures from Surveys of Students | | |
|---|---|---|
| Academic Support Among Peers | **Peer Classroom Behavior** measures the degree to which students' classmates treat each other with respect, work together well, and help each other learn, and if other students disrupt class, like to put others down, and don't care about each other. Students' reports refer to a specific class. | |
| | **Students' Sense of Belonging** measures students' reports of how personally connected they feel to the school. Students rate the degree to which the people at school feel like family, whether people at school care if they come to school, and whether they participate in activities at the school. | |
| | **Peer Support for Academic Achievement** asks students if their friends try hard in school, talk about classwork, help each other prepare for tests, and think it is important to attend classes. | |
| Classroom Climate | **Academic Engagement** examines student interest and engagement in learning. Students responded to items regarding whether they are interested in their class and the topics studied and work hard to do their best. Students' reports refer to a specific class. | |
| | **Classroom Personalism** gauges whether students perceive that their classroom teachers give them individual attention and show personal concern for them. Students were asked if their teachers know and care about them, notice if they are having trouble in class, and are willing to help with academic and personal problems. Students' reports refer to a specific class. | |
| | **Academic Press** measures whether teachers press all students toward academic achievement. Students were asked if their teacher expects them to do their best, expects everyone to work hard, if the work is difficult and challenging, if you have to work hard to do well, and if the teacher asks difficult questions. Students' reports refer to a specific class. | |
| Parent-Student Relationships | **Parent Support** for student learning gauges student views of their parents' support for their schoolwork. Students were asked about how often their parents (or other adults) encourage them to work hard, do their homework, and take responsibility. | |
| | **Parental Press** for academic achievement asks students about the frequency with which their parents or guardians talked to them about and encouraged them in their schoolwork. | |
| Safety and Discipline | **Incidence of Disciplinary Action** measures how often students get into trouble and are disciplined. Students were asked how many times they were sent to the office, how often their parents were contacted about discipline problems, and how often they had been suspended from school. | |
| | **Safety** reflects students' sense of personal safety inside and outside the school and traveling to and from school. | |

*Continued on next page*

**TABLE 3—CONTINUED**

**CCSR Measures on School Climate and Instruction**

| Measures from Surveys of Students | | |
|---|---|---|
| Schoolwide Orientation | **Importance of High School for the Future** includes questions about students' attitudes regarding the importance of high school, such as whether grades in high school matter for success in college, classes give useful preparation for what students' plan to do in life, if high school teaches valuable skills, whether what they learn in class is necessary for success in the future, and whether working hard in school matters for success in the workforce. | |
| | **Schoolwide Academic Press** for the future measures students' views of school norms of academic expectations. Students report on the degree to which all students are expected to work hard, stay in school, plan for their futures, and have high personal aspirations for their lives after graduation. | |
| School Resources | **Tech Hardware Availability** measures the extent to which students report computer hardware is available to them. | |
| | **School Clubs**, after-school activities measures the extent to which students at the school report participating in school clubs or after-school activities. | |
| | **Sports Teams** measures the extent to which students at the school participate in sports teams. | |
| | **Tutoring** measures the extent to which students at the school participate in after-school programs for help with schoolwork. | |
| Teacher-Student Relationships | **Student-Teacher Trust** focuses on the quality of relationships between students and teachers. Students were asked whether they believe teachers can be trusted, care about them, keep their promises, and listen to students' ideas, and if they feel safe and comfortable with their teachers. In high-scoring schools, there is a high level of care and communication between students and teachers. | |
| | **Teacher Personal Support** measures students' reports of teachers being there to help with personal matters. Students were asked whether there is a teacher who they can talk to about personal problems, who gives extra help with schoolwork, and who cares about how the student is doing. | |

| Measures from Surveys of Teachers | | |
|---|---|---|
| Coherence and Cooperation Among Teachers | **Instructional Program Coherence** assesses the degree to which teachers feel the programs at their school are coordinated with each other and with the school's mission. Teachers were asked if the materials in their schools are consistent both within and across grades, if there is sustained attention to quality program implementation, and if changes at the school have helped promote the school's goals for student learning. | |
| | **Collective Responsibility** focuses on the extent of shared commitment among the faculty to improve the school so that all students learn. Teachers were asked how many colleagues feel responsible for students' academic and social development, set high standards of professional practice, and take responsibility for school improvement. | |
| | **Reflective Dialogue** about practice reveals how much teachers talk with one another about instruction and student learning. Teachers reported how often they discuss curriculum and instruction as well as school goals, and how best to help students learn and how to manage their behavior. | |
| | **Teacher-Teacher Trust** measures the extent to which teachers in school have open communication with and respect for each other. We asked, for example, whether teachers in the school trust and respect each other feel like they can discuss feelings and frustrations. | |

*Continued on next page*

**TABLE 3–CONTINUED**
## CCSR Measures on School Climate and Instruction

| Measures from Surveys of Teachers | | |
|---|---|---|
| Classroom Practice | **Assignment Demand** asks teachers how often they require students to complete different types of assignments (e.g., short writing assignments of 1 or 2 pages, out-of-class readings, revisions of assignments). Teachers report about a specific class. | |
| | **Individualization of Instruction** asks teachers how often they adjust instructional strategies to respond to students' understanding, adjust pacing of a lesson, and modify their lessons to meet students' needs. Teachers report about a specific class. | |
| | **Personal Relationships with Students** asks teachers how often students talk to them about their friends, families, personal problems, their progress in class, academic achievements, and how they are doing in other classes. Teachers report about a specific class. | |
| | **Support of Testing and Learning Standards** asks teachers to what extent they align their teaching emphases with state learning standards, whether they believe the standards are appropriate guidelines, and whether test-score accountability has helped the school focus on what's best for students. | |
| Parent Interaction | **Teacher-Parent Interaction** measures teachers' reports of positive interactions with parents—whether parents support their teaching, do their best to help their children learn, and have confidence in teacher expertise; whether teachers and parents consider each other partners in educating children, and staff work to build trusting relationships with parents | |
| | **Teacher-Parent Trust** asks teachers whether they feel good about parents' support for their work, the extent to which they feel respected by their students' parents, whether teachers and parents think of each other as partners, whether staff work to build trusting relationships with parents, and whether parents have confidence in the expertise of teachers. | |
| Teachers' Feelings About the School | **Teacher Commitment to the School** gauges the extent to which teachers feel loyal and committed to the school. Teachers reported whether they look forward to working in the school, would rather work somewhere else, and would recommend the school to parents. | |
| | **Teacher Self-Efficacy** asks students how much they believe they can control disruptive behavior in the classroom, motivate students who show low interest, get students to believe they can do well in school work, and help students value learning. | |
| | **Teacher-Principal Trust** measures the extent to which teachers feel their principal respects them. Teachers were asked if their principal looks out for the welfare of teachers and has confidence in their expertise, and if they respect the principal as an educator. | |
| | **Expectations for Students Going to College** gauges whether teachers expect most students at the school to go to college, and help students plan for college, and if the curriculum is focused on getting students ready for college | |

*All measures come from the CCSR surveys conducted in Spring 2005. The survey items that were used to construct the measures, and the psychometric properties of the measures, are available at ccsr.uchicago.edu.*

# Appendix C: Correlations Involving Survey Measures

**TABLE 4**

**Significant School Correlations of Climate and Instruction with Student Outcomes**
Controlling for Student Backgrounds, Pre-High School Achievement, and School Composition

| Measures of Climate From Student Surveys | | Absences | Failures | GPA | Code* |
|---|---|---|---|---|---|
| Academic Support Among Peers | Peer Classroom Behavior | | | | PEER |
| | Students' Sense of Belonging | | | .23^ | BELS |
| | Peer Support for Academic Achievement | | -.20^ | .29* | PSAA |
| Classroom Climate | Academic Engagement | | -.24* | .24* | ENGG |
| | Classroom Personalism | -.28* | -.35** | .35** | PERC |
| | Academic Press | | | .22^ | PRES |
| Parent-Student Relationships | Parent Support for Student Learning | | | | PARS |
| | Parental Press for Academic Achievement | | | | PPAA |
| Safety and Discipline | Incidence of Disciplinary Action | | | | DISO |
| | Safety | -.22^ | | .22^ | SAFE |
| Schoolwide Orientation | Importance of High School for the Future | -.45*** | -.31* | .35** | FUTR |
| | Schoolwide Academic Press for the Future | -.43*** | -.36** | .47*** | SLAP |
| School Resources | Computer Availability | -.27* | | .22^ | SXAV |
| | School Clubs, After-School Activities | -.21^ | -.23^ | .35** | |
| | Sports Teams | -.22^ | -.24* | .27* | |
| | Tutoring | | | | |
| Teacher-Student Relationships | Student-Teacher Trust | -.40*** | -.40*** | .47*** | TRTS |
| | Teacher Personal Support | -.36** | -.27* | .37** | TSUP |

*****Code:** *These measure codes are provided for readers who would like to reference further information on measure construction by visiting the CCSR Web site at ccsr.uchicago.edu.*

*Continued on next page*

**TABLE 4–CONTINUED**

## Significant School Correlations of Climate and Instruction with Student Outcomes
Controlling for Student Backgrounds, Pre-High School Achievement, and School Composition

| Measures of Climate From Teacher Surveys | | Absences | Failures | GPA | Code* |
|---|---|---|---|---|---|
| Coherence and Cooperation | Instructional Program Coherence | -0.23^ | -0.26* | 0.25* | PGMC |
| | Collective Responsibility Among Teachers | -0.31* | | 0.25^ | COLR |
| | Reflective Dialogue About Practice | | | | REFD |
| | Teacher-Teacher Trust | | | 0.23^ | TRTE |
| Classroom Practice | Assignment Demand | | | | ADMD |
| | Individualization of Instruction | | | 0.24^ | INDV |
| | Personal Relationships with Students | | | | PERT |
| | Support of Testing and Learning Standards | 0.28* | 0.28* | -0.22^ | STND |
| Parent Interaction | Teacher-Parent Interaction | | | | TPIN |
| | Teacher-Parent Trust | | | | TRPA |
| Teachers' General Feelings | Teacher Commitment to the School | | | | SCMT |
| | Teacher Self-Efficacy | | | | TEFF |
| | Teacher-Principal Trust | | | | TRPR |
| | Expectations of Students Going to College | | | | UEXP |

^p<.10, *p<.05, **p<.01, ***p<.001

Correlations were calculated using residuals from two-level HLMs that predicted failures, absences, or grades with student-level demographic characteristics (gender, race, poverty, social status, school mobility in the three years before high school, age when began high school, days absent) and eighth-grade reading and math achievement, and two measures of student composition at the school level—average eighth-grade ITBS achievement of the freshman cohort, and average residential poverty level of the freshman cohort.

*Code: These measure codes are provided for readers who would like to reference further information on measure construction by visiting the CCSR Web site at ccsr.uchicago.edu.

**TABLE 5**

**Correlations of School Climate and Instruction with Student Composition**

| Measures of Climate From Student Surveys | | Average Incoming Achievement[1] | Poverty Level of Students[2] | Code* |
|---|---|---|---|---|
| Academic Support Among Peers | Peer Classroom Behavior | 0.61 *** | -0.69 *** | PEER |
| | Students' Sense of Belonging | 0.52 *** | -0.23 * | BELS |
| | Peer Support for Academic Achievement | 0.23 * | 0.17 | PSAA |
| Classroom Climate | Academic Engagement | -0.32 ** | 0.37 *** | ENGG |
| | Classroom Personalism | -0.23 * | 0.30 ** | PERC |
| | Academic Press | 0.09 | 0.19 | PRES |
| Parent-Student Relationships | Parent Support for Student Learning | -0.18 | 0.60 * | PARS |
| | Parental Press for Academic Achievement | 0.22 ^ | 0.04 | PPAA |
| Safety and Discipline | Incidence of Disciplinary Action | -0.73 *** | 0.63 *** | DISO |
| | Safety | 0.51 *** | -0.28 * | SAFE |
| Schoolwide Orientation | Importance of High School for the Future | 0.07 | 0.21 ^ | FUTR |
| | Schoolwide Academic Press for the Future | 0.31 ** | -0.16 | SLAP |
| School Resources | Computer Availability | 0.38 *** | -0.21 ^ | SXAV |
| | School Clubs, After-School Activities | 0.30 * | 0.14 | |
| | Sports Teams | 0.57 *** | -0.25 ^ | |
| | Tutoring | 0.05 | 0.08 | |
| Teacher-Student Relationships | Student-Teacher Trust | -0.05 | 0.00 | TRTS |
| | Teacher Personal Support | 0.22 ^ | 0.14 | TSUP |

| Measures of Climate From Teacher Surveys | | Average Incoming Achievement[1] | Poverty Level of Students[2] | Code* |
|---|---|---|---|---|
| Coherence and Cooperation | Instructional Program Coherence | 0.08 | -0.02 | PGMC |
| | Collective Responsibility Among Teachers | 0.19 | -0.19 | COLR |
| | Reflective Dialogue About Practice | 0.12 | 0.01 | REFD |
| | Teacher-Teacher Trust | 0.01 | 0.04 | TRTE |
| Classroom Practice | Assignment Demand | -0.36 | 0.48 *** | ADMD |
| | Individualization of Instruction | -0.06 | 0.12 | INDV |
| | Personal Relationships with Students | -0.05 | 0.12 | PERT |
| | Support of Testing and Learning Standards | -0.44 | 0.49 *** | STND |
| Parent Interaction | Teacher-Parent Interaction | -0.29 * | 0.24 ^ | TPIN |
| | Teacher-Parent Trust | 0.57 *** | -0.40 *** | TRPA |
| Teachers' General Feelings | Teacher Commitment to the School | 0.51 *** | -0.44 *** | SCMT |
| | Teacher Self-Efficacy | 0.23 ^ | 0.03 | TEFF |
| | Teacher-Principal Trust | 0.25 * | 0.00 | TRPR |
| | Expectations of Students Going to College | 0.52*** | -0.35 ** | UEXP |

*These are correlations without any adjustments for students' background characteristics.*
*^p<.10, *p<.05, **p<.01, ***p<.001*
[1] *Defined as the average incoming eighth-grade math score on the ITBS*
[2] *Defined as the aggregate poverty of students' residential census block groups, where poverty was measured as the percent of families below the poverty line and the male unemployment rate*
***Code:*** *These measure codes are provided for readers who would like to reference further information on measure construction by visiting the CCSR Web site at ccsr.uchicago.edu.*

# Appendix D: Summaries of Models

**TABLE 6**

### Coefficients from Full Model Predicting Course Absences

| Level 2 | Coefficient | T-ratio |
|---|---|---|
| Intercept | 8.925 | 33.886 *** |
| Average Incoming Achievement in School | -2.034 | -4.850 *** |
| Average Poverty Level in School | -0.142 | -0.425 |

| Level 1 | Coefficient | T-ratio |
|---|---|---|
| Male | 0.806 | 7.137 *** |
| African-American | -0.966 | -3.654 *** |
| American Indian | -0.032 | -0.022 |
| Asian | -2.774 | -7.597 *** |
| Latino | -1.397 | -5.872 *** |
| Poverty | 0.758 | 7.172 *** |
| Social Status | 0.091 | 0.916 |
| Moved Once in 3 Years Before High School | 0.944 | 7.430 *** |
| Moved Twice in 3 Years Before High School | 2.632 | 13.557 *** |
| Moved 3+ Times in 3 Years Before High School | 5.424 | 16.703 *** |
| Eighth-Grade Math ITBS Score | -0.048 | -16.820 *** |
| Eighth-Grade Reading ITBS Score | -0.008 | -3.087 ** |
| Began School Early | -1.852 | -4.445 *** |
| Slightly Old-for-Grade When Began High School | 0.275 | 2.070 * |
| Months Old-for-Grade When Began High School | 0.268 | 17.199 *** |

^$p<.10$, *$p<.05$, **$p<.01$, ***$p<.001$

*The variable representing absences is slightly skewed (skew=1.6). Models were also run on the log of absences, which has a normal distribution. However, the results were very similar so models using the untransformed outcome are displayed here for ease of interpretability.*

**TABLE 7**

### Variance Components from Models Predicting Course Absences (in Days)

| Model | Unexplained Level 1 Variance (Individual Level) | Unexplained Level 2 Variance (School Level) |
|---|---|---|
| 1. Unconditional | 86.0 | 18.8 |
| 2. With background characteristics plus student achievement at level 1 | 79.2 | 10.7 |
| 3. With background characteristics plus student achievement and school composition at level 2 | 71.5 | 4.9 |

**TABLE 8**

**Coefficients From Full Models Predicting Course Failure Rates**

| | Model without Freshman Attendance | | Model with Freshman Attendance | |
|---|---|---|---|---|
| **Level 2** | Coefficient | T-ratio | Coefficient | T-ratio |
| Intercept | 2.530 | 30.839 *** | 1.775 | 27.506 *** |
| Average Incoming Achievement in School | -0.416 | -3.166 ** | 0.196 | 1.921 |
| Average Poverty Level in School | -0.276 | -2.627 * | -0.240 | -2.924 ** |
| **Level 1** | Coefficient | T-ratio | Coefficient | T-ratio |
| Male | 1.006 | 22.440 *** | 0.644 | 20.096 *** |
| African-American | 0.128 | 1.222 | 0.387 | 5.365 *** |
| American Indian | 0.055 | 0.096 | 0.370 | 1.022 |
| Asian | -0.567 | -3.903 *** | 0.354 | 3.726 *** |
| Latino | 0.091 | 0.960 | 0.421 | 6.537*** |
| Poverty | 0.220 | 5.246 *** | -0.030 | -1.001 |
| Social Status | 0.008 | 0.212 | -0.050 | -1.825 |
| Moved Once in 3 Years Before High School | 0.293 | 5.801 *** | -0.004 | -0.102 |
| Moved Twice in 3 Years Before High School | 0.787 | 10.231 *** | -0.005 | -0.080 |
| Moved 3+ Times in 3 Years Before High School | 1.443 | 11.237 *** | -0.233 | -2.275 * |
| Eighth-Grade Math ITBS Score | -0.022 | -19.467 *** | -0.007 | -8.825 *** |
| Eighth-Grade Reading ITBS Score | -0.001 | -0.994 | 0.001 | 1.077 |
| Began School Early | -0.555 | -3.350 ** | 0.075 | 0.670 |
| Slightly Old-for-Grade When Began High School | 0.036 | 0.679 | -0.031 | -0.839 |
| Months Old-for-Grade When Began High School | 0.073 | 11.798 *** | 0.004 | 0.759 |
| Study Behaviors | | | -0.324 | -15.186 *** |
| Days Absent | | | 0.319 | 124.151 *** |

^p<.10, *p<.05, **p<.01, ***p<.001

**TABLE 9**

**Variance Components from Models Predicting Course Failure Rates**

| Model | Unexplained Level 1 Variance (Individual Level) | Unexplained Level 2 Variance (School Level) |
|---|---|---|
| 1. Unconditional | 12.43 | 1.16 |
| 2. With student background characteristics at level 1 | 11.80 | 0.78 |
| 3. With background characteristics plus student achievement at level 1 | 11.46 | 0.52 |
| 4. With background characteristics plus student achievement and school composition at level 2 | 11.45 | 0.46 |
| 5. With student background characteristics, achievement, school composition and freshman absence rates and studying | 3.44 | 0.26 |

**TABLE 10**

**Coefficients From Full Models Predicting GPA**

| Level 2 | Model without Freshman Attendance and Studying | | Model with Freshman Attendance and Studying | |
|---|---|---|---|---|
| | Coefficient | T-ratio | Coefficient | T-ratio |
| Intercept | 1.973 | 88.396 *** | 2.221 | 104.223 *** |
| Average Incoming Achievement in School | 0.138 | 3.860 *** | -0.063 | -1.886 |
| Average Poverty Level in School | 0.081 | 2.823 ** | 0.068 | 2.493 * |

| Level 1 | Coefficient | T-ratio | Coefficient | T-ratio |
|---|---|---|---|---|
| Male | -0.408 | -34.452 *** | -0.323 | -30.487 *** |
| African-American | -0.196 | -7.088 *** | -0.309 | -12.950 *** |
| American Indian | -0.062 | -0.411 | -0.130 | -1.087 |
| Asian | 0.375 | 9.79 *** | 0.100 | 3.186 ** |
| Latino | -0.109 | -4.373 ** | -0.208 | -9.756 *** |
| Poverty | -0.061 | -5.474 *** | -0.009 | -0.928 |
| Social Status | -0.002 | -0.191 | 0.000 | -0.009 |
| Moved Once in 3 Years Before High School | -0.079 | -5.929 *** | -0.003 | -0.275 |
| Moved Twice in 3 Years Before High School | -0.207 | -10.187 *** | -0.023 | -1.189 |
| Moved 3+ Times in 3 Years Before High School | -0.356 | -10.448 *** | 0.045 | 1.320 |
| Eighth-Grade Math ITBS Score | 0.009 | 30.691 *** | 0.006 | 22.980 *** |
| Eighth-Grade Reading ITBS Score | 0.001 | 2.587 | 0.001 | 2.770 ** |
| Began School Early | 0.225 | 5.148 *** | 0.048 | 1.313 |
| Months Old-for-Grade When Began High School | -0.021 | -12.955 *** | -0.003 | -2.385 * |
| Study Behaviors | | | 0.203 | 28.819 *** |
| Days Absent[1] | | | -0.083 | -97.154 *** |

^p<.10, *p<.05, **p<.01, ***p<.001

[1] For simplicity, days absent was entered in this model without transformation (although extreme values of greater than 40 were trimmed to 40). Because it is somewhat positively skewed, the models were re-run with the square root of absence, which has only a slight positive skew. The square root of absences showed a slightly stronger relationship with grades, and similar patterns were observed.

**TABLE 11**

**Variance Components from Models Predicting GPA**

| Model | Unexplained Level 1 Variance (Individual Level) | Unexplained Level 2 Variance (School Level) |
|---|---|---|
| 1. Unconditional | 1.01 | 0.18 |
| 2. With background characteristics plus student achievement at level 1 | 0.83 | 0.06 |
| 3. With background characteristics plus student achievement, absences, and study behaviors at level 1 | 0.38 | 0.04 |
| 4. With background characteristics plus student achievement and school composition at level 2 (not controlling for absences and study behaviors) | 0.79 | 0.03 |
| 5. With student background characteristics, achievement, school composition, freshman absence rates and study behaviors | 0.38 | 0.03 |

Appendix D

## About the Authors

### Elaine M. Allensworth

Elaine M. Allensworth is the Co-Director for Statistical Analysis at the Consortium on Chicago School Research at the University of Chicago (CCSR). She holds a Ph.D. in Sociology, and an M.A. in Sociology and Urban Studies from Michigan State University. Allensworth is an expert in statistical methodology, but believes that knowledge develops best by combining qualitative and quantitative methods. Her work focuses on the structural factors that affect high school students' educational attainment, particularly the factors that affect graduation and dropout rates. She was the lead author on a number of studies on graduation rates in the Chicago Public Schools, including *The On-Track Indicator as a Predictor of High School Graduation* (2005), *Graduation and Dropout Trends in Chicago: A look at cohorts of students from 1991 through 2004* (2005), and *Ending Social Promotion: Dropout Rates in Chicago after Implementation of the Eighth-Grade Promotion Gate* (2004). She recently began a three-year mixed-methods study of the transition to high school, which will follow a cohort of students from eighth grade into their second year in high school. This study looks at the ways in which students perceive the challenges of high school, the school practices that can foster successful freshman-year performance, and those that can hinder students. Allensworth is also a member of the CCSR postsecondary project, which is following students' transition from high school to college. As part of this work, she has been examining the factors affecting students' performance on the ACT. She is also leading several studies on the effects of rigorous curricula on students' experiences in their classes, grades, test scores, high school graduation, and college attendance. Allensworth was once a high school teacher.

### John Q. Easton

John Q. Easton is Executive Director of the Consortium. He has been affiliated with CCSR since its inception in 1990 and led its first research study. Much of Easton's research at CCSR examines trends in achievement test scores and the use of test scores in school improvement and school accountability efforts. He is coauthor of a recent study on the relationship between freshman-year academic performance and high school graduation. Easton holds a PhD in Measurement, Evaluation, and Statistical Analysis from the University of Chicago.

*This report reflects the interpretation of the authors. Although the Consortium's Steering Committee provided technical advice and reviewed earlier versions, no formal endorsement by these individuals, organizations, or the full Consortium should be assumed.*

*This report was produced by the Consortium's publications and communications staff.*

Editing and project management by the University Publications Office
Graphic Design by Jeff Hall Design
Photos by John Booz

# Consortium on Chicago School Research

## Directors

**John Q. Easton**
*Executive Director*
Consortium on Chicago
School Research

**Elaine Allensworth**
Consortium on Chicago
School Research

**Melissa Roderick**
University of Chicago

**Penny Bender Sebring**
Consortium on Chicago
School Research

## Steering Committee

**George Lowery,** *Co-chair*
Roosevelt University

**Josie Yanguas,** *Co-chair*
Illinois Resource Center

### Institutional Members

**Clarice Berry**
Chicago Principals and
Administrators Association

**Daniel T. Bugler**
**Barbara Eason-Watkins**
**Christy Harris**
Chicago Public Schools

**Marilyn Stewart**
Chicago Teachers Union

### Individual Members

**Gina Burkhardt**
Learning Point Associates

**Elizabeth Hawthorne**
Change Consultancy

**Timothy Knowles**
Center for Urban School
Improvement

**Janet Knupp**
Chicago Public
Education Fund

**Mark Larson**
National Louis University

**Carol D. Lee**
Northwestern University

**Deidra Lewis**
City Colleges of Chicago

**Peter Martinez**
University of Illinois
at Chicago

**Ruanda Garth McCullough**
Loyola University

**Samuel Meisels**
Erikson Institute

**James Pellegrino**
University of Illinois
at Chicago

**Stephen Raudenbush**
University of Chicago

**James Spillane**
Northwestern University

**Kim Zalent**
Business Professional People
for the Public Interest

**Steve Zemelman**
Illinois Network of
Charter Schools

**Martha Zurita**
Latino Youth Alternative
High School

## Our Mission

The Consortium on Chicago School Research (CCSR) at the University of Chicago aims to conduct research of high technical quality that can inform and assess policy and practice in the Chicago Public Schools. By broadly engaging local leadership in our work, and presenting our findings to diverse audiences, we seek to expand communication among researchers, policy makers, and practitioners. CCSR encourages the use of research in policy action, but does not argue for particular policies or programs. Rather, we believe that good policy is most likely to result from a genuine competition of ideas, informed by the best evidence that can be obtained.